I shall pass through
this world but once.
Any good therefore
that I can do or any
kindness that I can
show to any human
being, let me do it now.
Let me not defer or
neglect it for I shall
not pass this way
again.

EX LIBRIS

Nichols

THE MARX BROTHERS
BROTHERS
THEIR WORLD OF COMEDY

THE MARX BROTHERS
THEIR WORLD OF COMEDY

by ALLEN EYLES

South Brunswick
New York: A.S. Barnes and Co.

Acknowledgements

The author is particularly indebted to David S. Parlett for the many comments and suggestions he has made to improve the manuscript from his own detailed knowledge of the Marx Brothers; and to George Joseph Folsey, who photographed the earliest Marx Brothers' films, for providing certain reminiscences.

Almost all of the stills have been generously loaned by Bo Johan Hultman and John Kobal from their collections.

Thanks are given to the following for providing information and other forms of assistance: Kevin Brownlow; Kingsley Canham; Paul Chown; John Cutts; Ted Gilling; John Hickey; Jim Kearley; Mrs. Doris McChesney; and Barrie Pattison. The Classic Cinemas deserve mention for cultivating the author's interest in the Marx Brothers through constant revivals of their films during the fifties. Additional illustrations came from the British Film Institute's Stills Library and through the magazine *films and filming* (Robin Bean), while the B.F.I.'s Information Department yielded much factual material.

Contents

Superior numbers in the text correspond to entries in the Bibliography.

1. Introduction

They are the most heroic of all the screen comedians. They tackle a world that obstructs them and bring it to submission as capably as a cowboy hero disposes of the villains. The comic personalities before the Marxes, in the period of silent cinema, were people of innocence, stoic or sentimental, small figures in a large and hostile universe who perhaps mastered their fate but only by chance, luck, or plodding determination. Chaplin was a little more aspiring cheekily seizing on opportunities, but becoming awkwardly too aware of himself and too conceited. The lack of size of these comedians fitted their lowly place in the world on the screen.

The team are the heroes of everyone who has suffered from other people's hypocrisy, pomposity, pedantism, and patronage. They settle for none of it. The Marxes assume that we join them on their comic crusade. They don't need us but they treat us as equals and invite us to side with them. This is what is implied when Groucho takes the trouble to pause and have a few friendly words in his asides. He shares his thoughts, offers friendly advice, or apologises for a bad joke, but the other lot — *they* ignore us completely, besides which they make no more favourable an impression on us than they do on the Marxes.

It is also easier to identify with Groucho because he is the one who enters society and meets its situations as we have to. He only superficially belongs to it, for his ill-fitting garments and greasepaint moustache are only to get him past the door and he could easily throw them aside (whereas Chaplin certainly doesn't need to dress up for the social strata in which he moves — his similar appearance shows an attempt to live up to society, accepting its standards by wearing somebody's castoffs). However, in other ways, Harpo is perhaps the most human for there is an underlying consistency about what he does, his actions seeming to be an authentic part of a total character. As a performer, Harpo impresses his own personality on his routines. He is less of a puzzle, more immediately comprehensible than Groucho, even though his special powers and near infallibility make him also somewhat super-human. Groucho is so busy striking attitudes and being inconsistent that there are few moments when he is at repose, his relaxed self. In action at any rate, he might be classified as parahuman. Chico must be regarded as virtually sub-human with his dense ways; and Zeppo is, on screen, about half-human, half-wooden. This variety of character is a great asset of the Marxes, as it was in the case of the British team of Will Hay, Moore Marriott and Graham Moffatt. But too many comedy teams have tended to be too alike, with one simply made more stupid to act as a butt.

Zeppo, the fourth Marx Brother, is not so interesting, but he is worth having for all his awkwardness just because he is one of the family. He deserves a place and the family solidarity his presence expresses is rather likable — to know of the fifth brother, Gummo, is to regret that he was never around on screen. This solidarity is slow in coming and sometimes only fleeting, for it takes time for the Marxes to forget their screen differences and come together as the family group that underneath we know them to be.

The Marxes then are big figures with a zest for life and nothing to fear from it. They refuse to need any sympathy from us. With most of the great clowns, we laugh *at* them, at their physical discomfort, at their setbacks and humiliations. How much better it is that we can laugh *with* the Marx Brothers — at deserving targets. (When, later on, they do become briefly gloomy and dejected, we feel for them because they are our heroes, and because we know what a comedown it is from their usual performance.)

The Marxes have much in common with the other most important comic personalities of their time: Mae West and W.C. Fields. In their cynicism, worldliness and lack of heart, all matched the bitter mood of the Depression. Appearing in the most hackneyed stories, Mae West joked directly with the audience about sex — her whole ample figure was a joke about it. (The Marxes have similar fun with notions of love and sex, but are not seriously interested in it as it would compromise their independence. The team's lack of respect for the opposite sex rarely endears them or their work to its members.) W. C. Fields was a down-trodden, shifty, half-rejected or half-defeated figure who contrived to cock an occasional snook at society in a personal gesture of defiance and revenge. But with the Marx Brothers *all* the barricades of society went down (except one totally ignored — religion. Small children should perhaps also be included, but one wouldn't give much for Babe LeRoy's chances crossing swords with a Marx brother). Perhaps the nearest thing on the same scale in the thirties were the subsequent epic blunders of Will Hay, Moore Marriott and Graham Moffatt in the British cinema, but these lack the cut and thrust of the Marx work, being in the British tradition of 'bungling through'. The comic disasters deliberately caused by the Marxes have no parallel.

Comedians, it is said, must have 'heart' and lack greatness without pathos. Having it can certainly be a considerable fault (*vide* Norman Wisdom, Jerry Lewis); not having it, with the Marxes, becomes a distinct virtue. When that whole, tired and rather selfishly demanding theory is overthrown, the dignified independence of the Marx Brothers should be very highly rated. It is also sometimes suggested that the Marxes' work is 'uncinematic', that they fail to use the full possibilities of the medium. This is to miss the point: the Marxes set the pace, and the camera's function is merely to catch their actions as unobtrusively as possible, not to restrict their freedom. The humour belongs to the Marxes and is best left unpolished by the finer tricks of style.

The juvenile chirpiness of Lloyd, the plucky determination of Keaton, the crass incompetence and superb bluffing of Will Hay (contrasting with the senile cunning of Moore Marriott), the fore-doomed misadventures of Laurel and Hardy — all these are to be prized, but this book is written from the viewpoint that the Marxes' work is the most fascinating, most subtle, and most rewarding of all that done by the various comic personalities.

2. Background

W e need first to look at the background from which the Marx films came. It is true that the Marx Brothers' early lives have been very fully documented with only a few discrepancies emerging. All the accounts regrettably give little space to the period when the films were made, so a few outside references to the experience of working with the team are included here. Before giving a brief outline of how they developed prior to the films, it might be useful to sum up the further background material. Kyle Crichton's book [3], the earliest, is the most compact and comprehensive; Harpo's [14] the most warmly human; and Groucho's [11] the most discursive and candid Arthur Marx has written a lightweight volume about his father, Groucho, that adds some further details.[10]

The Marxes' mother, Minnie Schoenberg, came to New York from Germany with her parents when she was 15. Three years later she married another immigrant, a Sam Marx from Alsace. Their eldest son, Leonard (later Chico), was born on March 22, 1891, and died at the age of 70 on October 11, 1961. He was followed by Adolph (later Arthur, finally Harpo), who was born on November 23, 1893, and died aged 70 on September 28, 1964; then Julius (to become Groucho), on October 2, 1895; Herbert (nicknamed Zeppo), on February 25, 1901; and finally a brother not seen in any film, Milton (Gummo). The family settled in a German-Jewish district on Manhattan Island.

Minnie's parents, who lived with them, gave the family a theatrical tradition. In Germany they had been travelling entertainers, the father a ventriloquist-cum-magician, his wife playing the harp after his performances for the audience to dance. Minnie's brother, Al Shean, was the entertainer of her generation and the big celebrity of the Marx clan. It was through Minnie's efforts that he originally became a vaudeville star for she badgered the bookers and got him dates just as she was to do for her own sons.

Observing the early rebuffs of her children on their own, Minnie consolidated them into a single vaudeville act, excepting Chico who was making a fair success of himself. Groucho and Gummo sang together with a hired performer and were joined by Harpo around 1909, then by Minnie and a relative. Groucho played the guitar during the act (as he does later in some films) while Gummo and Harpo performed on mandolins. There was no great demand for the act.

The day they switched from music to comedy was around 1914, and they largely copied a skit, *Fun In Hi Skule* or *School Days*, that they had seen elsewhere. Harpo wore his red wig for the first time. Chico joined up with them and he added a piano piece to their brash routines (which, to judge by the extracts quoted in their books, had hints of their later work, and much the same spirit as the biology class in *Horse Feathers*). Harpo, a little envious of Chico's piano, experimented with a harp and soon had it in the act. More horseplay slipped into the show whenever Minnie wasn't looking and the musical half was eventually abandoned in favour of more comedy. In one new scene Harpo relates that he had a line when he announced himself as the garbage man. Groucho retorted, "Sorry, we don't need any." The same idea occurs in *The Cocoanuts* ("There's a man outside wants to see you with a black moustache," Groucho is told and says, "Tell him I've got one"). Less tersely expressed, Groucho still uses the gag in 1965, telling an interviewer: "This morning I am awakened by a great din and am told it's the dustman. I told him to get lost. Who needs dust?"

At about this stage in their career, a fellow performer handed out their enduring nicknames along with the cards he was dealing in a poker game: 'Harpo' for obvious reasons; 'Chico' for his amorous pursuit of 'chicks'; 'Groucho' either for his grouchy outlook, always scenting disaster, or because he kept his money in a 'grouchbag'; and 'Gummo' either from the gumboots he invariably wore or because he sneaked up on people as though wearing them. 'Zeppo' was a family gift variously explained — see Kyle Crichton's Chapter 14 — and made when he finished schooling and replaced Gummo who had enlisted.

The troupe were still not offering a very distinguished show and Chico's enthusiasm did a lot to keep them going. They were good but they needed the overhauling Al Shean gave their work. The improvement made them a great success. Chico was firmly a dialect comedian, and Harpo was a pantomimist because he hadn't been given any lines (before this he had been a fairly typical 'idiot boy' but he did much better mute and devising his own material). About this time, he had not only the red wig but the familiar plug hat and underslung pants. He added the trench-coat that was to stay with him through all his films, stacked up with valuable props 'like the caverns of Ali-Baba' [9]. Also, he introduced the bulb-shaped taxicab horn which sounded when someone bumped into him. His familiar screen appearance had at this stage been virtually evolved through trial and error. (But in Hollywood Harpo was given a screen test at M-G-M and failed dismally.) Groucho, too, had moved part of the way to his screen character, substituting a grease-paint moustache for the old crepe one.

Harpo's routine of the stolen cutlery cascading out of his sleeve at an inopportune moment such as when he is shaking a policeman's hand was also worked out at about this time; it forms part of the first two Marx films, and Harpo was still using it on television appearances in the late fifties.

All the Marxes needed was to progress beyond vaudeville. They were forced into this when they fell out of favour with the powers in the profession and signed in desperation for a tatty musical show called *I'll Say She Is* (like that of several early films, the title is simply a popular saying). The Marxes' talent kept the show running an incredible seventeen weeks in the slack summer season (before air-conditioning) at a Philadelphia theatre. They put in eighteen months on the road before they could cajole the producers to open it on Broadway as the terms of their contract gave them the right to insist. The team's debut in this show on May 19, 1924, paid off in rave notices. After all the years of polishing their techniques and fashioning an attitude to comedy, they had met with a script (by Will B. Johnstone) that provided a firm basis for them to establish a world of comedy. All the details described and the photographs available suggest that this was fully a Marx show. As such, it is the only one that is not preserved on film.

The real world outside had given up its opposition to their efforts, and for the Marxes there was no turning back. Yet they had a few bad moments when their new show, *The Cocoanuts*, opened disastrously out of town: but at any rate it was a great success when it arrived in New York late in 1925. (The Marxes seem to have been dogged by this kind of temporary setback: even using identical material, they could click with one audience, not with another. They needed a certain sympathy for their style. Even their films — tried classics like *A Night at the Opera* — in London-area revivals could be a buoyantly entertaining experience eliciting roars of laughter at one theatre but seem an unfathomable mystery watched almost in silence at another. The predominant mood of the audience varied. The Marx brothers are always playing for (but not to) a crowd, which is why solitary televiewing of the Marx films isn't to be recommended.)

The Cocoanuts ran a full season on Broadway, then went on tour. *Animal Crackers* opened next and shortly afterwards Minnie Marx, seeing her sons safely at the top, left them to carry on, dying at the age of 65. (Their father, Sam Marx, survived her and even makes an appearance as an extra in *A Night at the Opera* — he must be the impeccably dressed gentleman with the thin moustache standing behind Allan Jones as he sings at the dockside to the departing heroine.)

While *Animal Crackers* was running, the Marxes went out to the Astoria Studios on Long Island to shoot the film version of *The Cocoanuts*. After running its full season, the show recessed for the summer, then went on tour in the autumn in 1929. Soon after, the great Wall Street crash occurred. The Marxes did no more stage shows.

After filming *Animal Crackers*, they went to Hollywood to make screen originals, the first of which was *Monkey Business*. Their film career had in fact started at the end of an era.

What kind of a period was it when the Marxes came out on top? It was the time between the First World War and the Depression — little more than a decade. Popularly, it is a period of riotous living called the Gay Twenties.

For humour, the twenties was less a distinct period — more a time of transition. A very significant date is February 21, 1925, when the *New Yorker*, styling itself partly on *Punch*, came into existence through the efforts of newspaperman Harold Ross. The previous May the Marxes had opened in *I'll Say She Is*, and established themselves; the December after publication started, the Marxes opened in *The Cocoanuts* and clinched matters. So the two came before the public eye at about the same time. Whereas the *New Yorker* stood at the pole of sophistication and genteel humour, the Marxes were based on its antipodes, being coarse, outrageous anti-sophisticates in their comedy. But the two were linked in many respects and between them lay the spectrum of progressive humour for the next decade. They had pretty much the same audience and made all kinds of allusions that they never explained; neither advocated anything, both mocked and satirised what existed. The *New Yorker* also did its best to promote the Marx Brothers, printing Alexander Woollcott's profile of Harpo and regularly reporting on the antics, offstage and on, of the quartet.

A common meeting ground was the legendary Algonquin Round Table, "a journalistic bohemia, given to uninhibited horseplay and ribald wit" where "it was sometimes hard to tell where juvenility left off and sophistication began." [32] Here the Marx Brothers, especially Harpo, could be found; here also could be discovered the literary wits — Woollcott, George S. Kaufman, Dorothy Parker, Robert Benchley, and many others, including Ross himself.

The *New Yorker* quickly became pre-eminent in its field, but were the Marxes correspondingly pre-eminent in the theatre? To the veteran critic John Mason Brown, making an impromptu recollection of Broadway at this time [25], one conclusion was clear. "The twenties, regrettably clownish as they were in other respects, were theatrically notable as a period of great clowns. The zanies who then stalked the stage were titans. The roster was an incredible one." He names first of all "the Marx Brothers (really meaning Harpo and Groucho), who by their monkeyshines in *Animal Crackers* made the kind of Marxists of us all that would have won Senator McCarthy's approval." Many of the other comics he then goes on to mention — Ed Wynn, Bobby Clark, Jimmy Durante, Victor Moore, Joe Cook, Willie Howard, Charles Butterworth, "all of them old soldiers in the good cause of laughter who refuse to die away" — are familiar enough from their film work but none of them can rank with the Marx Brothers. None had vehicles shaped for them in the way that the Marxes did or leave work that survives as the Marxes' work does. Most of them are best remembered for their supporting work in films which they didn't dominate. In fact it is other names altogether — W. C. Fields, and Will Hay in Britain particularly come to mind — who might be ranked with the Marx Brothers. They are considered later in the section on the Marx Brothers' place in cinema, but we might note here that they, and other names of interest, (like Bert Kalmar and Harry Ruby, also Bob Hope) had the same background as the Marxes had originally: vaudeville or music hall. As far as the theatre and real recognition went, the Marxes seem to have been the giants of the period.

Today success or failure is often determined much earlier in life and there is scant room for a gradual realisation of latent talents such as the Marx Brothers' numerous years on the vaudeville circuits provided. They switched from vaudeville to the legitimate stage really by chance. *I'll Say She Is* just bridged the gap in classification between 'tab show' and full-fledged musical comedy. Once on the stage, they were taken up by the cinema at a time when the techniques for making sound pictures helped to ensure that the stage shows were largely filmed as they stood. Looking at *The Cocoanuts* and *Animal Crackers* today, we have the rare experience of seeing a permanent record of the Broadway twenties and an impression of the vaudeville beyond that. Even if we find these films unamusing, we are looking at productions that were a mass delight and two of the great Broadway successes of the period. And we see four comedians making a nimble leap from the last days of vaudeville to the first days when the cinema was properly equipped to accept them.

3. The Cocoanuts (1929)

The Marx Brothers' first picture is certainly one of their best. It differs quite substantially from the later Paramount pictures by having a rather ponderous framework of romance, plot, and musical numbers. Two big musical comedy stars of the period, Mary Eaton and Oscar Shaw, receive co-star billing with the Marxes and get the final close-up. Just as in their later M-G-M pictures, the team helps to smooth the path of true love and the film is a 'well-balanced' entertainment. (Even at the time the critics weren't fully appreciative — one wrote: "The picture is not always interesting, in fact the sappy musical plot becomes downright boring at times". The original show, too, has the reputation of being the only one on which Irving Berlin worked that failed to give him a hit number.) At any rate, for the rest of their career at Paramount, the Marx Brothers earned the right to have the whole picture to themselves and didn't have to step aside for anyone.

The quartet don't seem to have had much help in this new medium. Of their two directors, Groucho said recently: "One of them didn't understand English, the other didn't understand Harpo". This refers to Robert Florey and Joseph Santley respectively. Florey says [30] that Santley merely collaborated on the musical numbers, and Florey's own interest seems to have been focussed there. He mentions thinking out the overhead shot where, in Busby Berkeley fashion, the dancers open out into a floral pattern, but he also mentions devising business for Harpo. The director of photography, George Folsey, thinks that Florey didn't really appreciate the Marx type of humour at that time. Neither did the studio bosses with whom Groucho had to argue to wear his painted moustache and later to talk to the audience. To add to the difficulties of film-making in early sound days (Groucho and Margaret Dumont seem to have gone through lines so many times that they make audible slips in delivery such as happens in no later film), the Marxes themselves made a problem. Florey recalls that they were never all available: Harpo spent his time making jokes and running after girls; Chico would either be on the studio roof or down in the basement; Zeppo came late; and Groucho would make interminable speeches. Like W.C. Fields, the Marx Brothers seemed to have treated Hollywood with no consideration at all and it is this uninhibited approach to life that shines through their screen performances, giving them that extra sense of conviction.

The Cocoanuts ran as much as 140 minutes at a preview but was

THE COCOA—
NUTS: "Do you
know that pro-
perty values have
increased 1929
since 1000%?"
Margaret Dumont
as Mrs. Potter
eyes Groucho's
map when he
starts to lecture
her on Florida.

cut back to 96 minutes for release. The print that MCA-TV have sent
out for television was obviously put together with considerable difficulty from a number of battered negatives or old prints, and runs
about 92 minutes when projected theatrically. It is more than long
enough for Groucho, Chico and Harpo to deliver a substantial amount
of fine comedy between the interventions of the singing lovers, the
jewel thieves, and the dancers. Zeppo, the fourth brother, has less to
do here than in the later films — which is surprising. His part may
have been reduced in cutting but as the film stands he merely ac-
knowledges remarks made by Groucho and prefaces Groucho's arrival at the party which forms the last scene in the film.

*   *   *

Groucho appears in *The Cocoanuts* as Mr. Hammer (no fuller
name), the owner-manager of a 600-room hotel in Florida. The background is the boom in property values that took place in Florida
during the twenties. Groucho also owns some surrounding real estate
which he auctions during the film. His name derives from the auc-

THE COCOA—
NUTS: Groucho,
behind the counter,
watches as a page
boy tries to take the
suitcase from the
two guests. A mo-
ment later, it is
revealed to be empty
but Chico has plans
to fill it before
leaving.

tioneer's hammer but it rather lacks the colourfulness of his later ones. In general, Groucho is the Marx brother who has some kind of temporary foothold in society, a position reached by trickery or misunderstanding. (Zeppo is usually related to him in some way, here as the hotel's desk clerk; Harpo and Chico are on the very fringe of society if not outsiders.) But it is rather odd to find Groucho actually a property owner. He normally lives for the moment, a parasite on society, and the thought of his taking a permanent stake in society and persevering in any work like running a hotel is alien to Groucho's overall character. It is more plausible when we discover that he is utterly broke, but then there is still hope for him as the season has yet to open. Still, there are many guests and Groucho is so incapable (and indifferent) that only one of them is paying her hotel fees. And Mrs. Potter is so very proper a woman that she wouldn't dream of overlooking it.

As Mrs. Potter, we find Margaret Dumont making the first of her seven appearances in the Marx world. Here she is seen at her most ample, a broadly streamlined figure in lace-dress and wide-brimmed, floppy hat, with an eye-glass for keeping life at a distance. The scene where Groucho — by contrast, a small, darting figure — grapples

THE COCOA-NUTS: Groucho grapples with the cumbersome bulk of Margaret Dumont's Mrs. Potter.

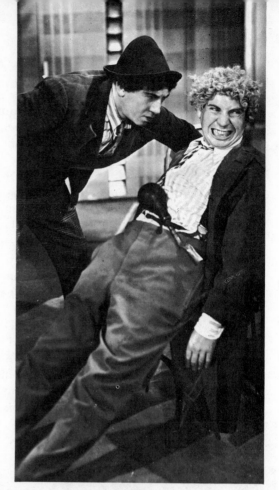

Left, THE COCOANUTS: Harpo is not amused. Dressed for the
party scene, he makes this expression on hearing the speeches.
Right , ANIMAL CRACKERS: Harpo is told to come out fighting.
His unsuspecting opponent in Margaret Dumont as Mrs. Rittenhouse.

with her cumbersome bulk is a visual expression of much of the
satire in the Marx films. She represents stuffy, narrow, hidebound
society (and never more so than in *The Cocoanuts*). She is impervious to any attack on her inborn sense of dignity and calm. True,
she can often be seen looking a little dubious or bewildered by the
Marx Brothers and she even complains once or twice, but she always
manages to overlook their actions and assume the best — she cannot
conceive that they could possibly mean to be rude.

Margaret Dumont was trained for the stage and played this part in
the Broadway production. She makes no adjustment for the change
of medium, and her delivery and expressions are all overscaled as
though she were still on stage. This serves to make her all the more
ridiculous and all the more inviting a target. Beyond this, Groucho
maintains that she didn't actually understand many of the jokes
directed at her, which can only have served to make her perfor-

mance even more effective. In her other work, she generally played the same role of the rich dowager, but she never registered as well as she did with the Marx Brothers where she contrasted so superbly with the team. Appendix I deals with Margaret Dumont and her career in more detail.

In *The Cocoanuts* there are some delightful glimpses of Mrs. Potter's closed mind. Her daughter Polly (played by Mary Eaton) is in love with a hotel clerk Bob Adams (Oscar Shaw) who has hopes of becoming an architect. This doesn't impress Mother. "One who clerks, Polly, is a clerk," she says with finality, adding, "And I

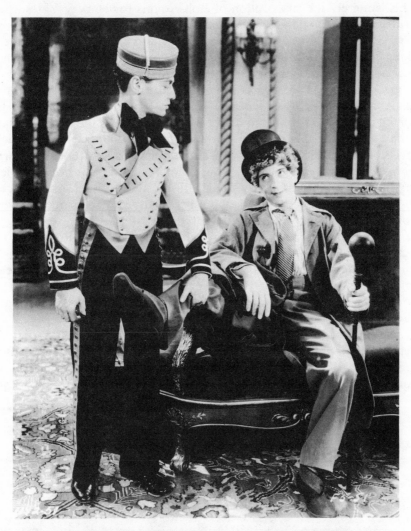

THE COCOANUTS: Harpo relaxes in the hotel lobby.

21

want you to remember that no Potter has ever been involved in a single scandal." A little cheekily, her daughter asks, "What about Uncle Dick?" "Polly," replies Mrs. Potter in her most insistent voice, "It is a well-known fact that your uncle was drunk at the time." Later on, she is the first to believe Bob guilty of stealing her necklace when the real thief, Penelope, tries to frame him. To wipe out the shame of her daughter's association with him, she promptly announces that Polly will marry Penelope's accomplice, Harvey Yates, of whom she approves because he is "one of the Boston Yates". Later, when Yates has been exposed in his true colours, she makes what she is able to call "a slight change" in the nuptial arrangements. This is merely the substitution of Bob Adams for Harvey Yates as the bridegroom, about the most radical change that could be made. But Mrs. Potter must maintain appearances and so she smooths everything over. Not incidentally, Bob Adams has suddenly become a most successful architect with his plan for developing the area.

Groucho tackles Margaret Dumont because her sense of self-importance and her excessive wealth (merely inherited, not earned) ask for it. It doesn't seem too unfair for she won't miss the odd few thousand and is well able to survive the let-down. Besides which, Groucho levels with her as he plays on her emotions. As she foolishly warms to his blandishments, he can't resist puncturing her illusions and letting her know what he really thinks. In the midst of a romantic scene in *Animal Crackers,* he puts it bluntly: "You have got money, haven't you? If not, we can quit right now."

Typical of the romantic hogwash he feeds Mrs. Potter is this remark, said as he tries to hold her tenderly. "Just think, tonight, tonight, when the moon is sneaking around the clouds, I'll be sneaking around you. I'll meet you tonight under the moon. Oh, I can see you now. You and the moon." After a pause he adds: "You wear a necktie so I'll know you."

The idea of love is constantly coarsened and vulgarised (notice the verb 'sneaking' in the above). Groucho elaborates on their future together: "... an empty bungalow just for me and you, where we could bill and cow — no, we could bull and cow ..." Groucho gets

more confused and gives up, but his words have linked the idea of love to crude animal sex. (In the preview-length print of the film, Groucho sang a number entitled 'A Little Bungalow'.)

In every encounter with Margaret Dumont, Groucho manages to insult her physical appearance. Penelope, the jewel thief, likens Harpo and Chico to the Prince of Wales as part of a scheme to frame them. The idea spreads and we come across Groucho making love to Mrs. Potter. "Did anyone ever tell you you look like the Prince of Wales? I don't mean the present Prince of Wales. One of the old Wales. And, believe me, when I say whales I mean whales. I know a whale when I see one."

As Groucho tries to take their courtship a stage further and embrace her, even she finds him a bit too much to tolerate. "Can't you keep your hands to yourself!" she exclaims as Groucho clumsily attempts to get a firm hold on her, whereupon he leaps back with his hands up, crying, "Come on, I'll play you one more game! The three of you!" This tender human situation has degenerated into some kind of vulgar sport and Margaret Dumont has been given the dimensions of three people. (In *Duck Soup* Groucho likens her bulk to an office block which needs to be torn down.)

Naturally Groucho loses no opportunity to expound his plans for developing the area to a wealthy widow. To really impress Mrs. Potter he produces a length of sewer pipe. "Look at it, nobody can fool you on a sewer pipe, can they, a woman like you?" Thus, at the same time as he flatters her as a woman of experience, he insults her by the type of experience he implies. He goes on to tell her that the size of pipe is not yet fixed and house-holders will be able to vote on it. If there's a tie, it will go to the Supreme Court, and Groucho happens to have inside information. *"The Chief Justice is crazy about this type sewer,"* he whispers in about the most way-out confidence even he has imparted — after which he walks off leaving her holding the sewer pipe, protesting in vain.

Part of Groucho's commanding manner comes from his presumption of being able to think for the other person as well. He assumes a belief that Mrs. Potter would like to know about Florida and so proceeds to lecture her. She manages to protest that he's told her before, but he answers that he left out a comma, a double absurdity not only because a comma can't be discerned in speech but also because it wouldn't rank a sufficient excuse for repeating everything if it was left out. "You know how alligator pears are made?" he inquires. She hasn't the slightest idea, or by the sound of it the slightest interest. "There you are!" declares Groucho, "That's because you couldn't have been an alligator and don't let it happen again. You know that it sometimes requires years to bring the alligator and the pear together? They don't like each other." Mrs. Potter is surprised. "No — you know how many alligator pears are

THE COCOANUTS: A rowdy moment in the hotel lobby as Groucho strips for action against Harpo and is restrained by Zeppo, calmed by Chico.

sent out of this state every year and told not to come back? All they can get hold of. Florida feeds the nation but nobody feeds me and that's what I want to talk to you about . . ." Groucho's remarks may be nonsense but they have a rich power of suggestion. In fact there are so many richly allusive ideas and techniques of verbal humour buried in Groucho's best dialogue that it is impossible at the time to fully unravel what he is saying. It is the fleeting impressions made on the mind that count. But if we pause for once to take them more slowly, we can see how he triggers off: a comparison between Mrs. Potter and an alligator (yet another suggestion that she is sub-human); the thought of alligators and pears as people, and as people not liking each other; then, putting the two together again, the idea that the exported alligator pear is a banished criminal. Besides all this, he has worked neatly around to his perennial concern with his own well-being.

At other times the power of Groucho's words lies not so much in the images they spark off but just in their sound. Groucho faces a demand for wages by his staff. He starts, as in the case of alligator pears, by misinterpreting a compound noun (wage slaves), and goes on to suggest vaguely a patriotic appeal and a quick bargain. This unbeatable combination has the staff cheering him. "Wages?" he asks them. "You want to be wage slaves? Answer me that." They don't. "No, of course not! Well, what makes wage slaves? Wages! I want you to be free. Remember, there's nothing like liberty except *Colliers* and the *Saturday Evening Post*. Be free, my friends, one for all and all for me and me for you and three for five and six for a quarter." The last line is a really inspired chain with a cumulative rhythm that makes it *sound* logical. It is bound together by the repetition of three-word phrases with the middle word "for", by the rhyming, and by the numerical increase. It starts with one stock phrase "one for all" and ends on another, "six for a quarter".

In a later scene, Groucho is trying to auction a lot and receiving no bids. "What am I offered for Lot 25 and a year's subscription to Youth Companion?" he asks. "Will somebody take a year's subscription, I'm trying to work my way through college?" Silence. "Will somebody take a six-months subscription — I'll go to high school. Does anybody want to buy a lead pencil? I'll wrestle anybody in the crowd for five dollars." This plays on the American ideal of self-advancement (working through college) and a familiar strategy of salesmanship stretched to absurdity. There is a deceptive sense of logic in the reduction of one year to six months paralleled by the lowering of college to high school. By contrast, there is nothing deceptive when Groucho yokes haircuts and eyesight together in flattering the bidders – there is obviously no connection between the two and this is ridiculously rather than cleverly amusing. Again, when Groucho links the highest bid to astigmatism, he levels with the customers (as he did earlier crying "Step up for the big swindle!").

Groucho so misuses the clichés of form and expression that they stand exposed for the tricks of argument they so often are. He uses emotionally coloured phrases in the wrong context, false analogies and false syllogisms, or merely a false way of pronouncing a word or phrase, to show how easily lucid thought and communication can be bedevilled.

A great achievement of these early films is how consistently phrases and words right for this treatment come up, triggering off powerful reactions that we respond to automatically. As time went on, this gift was lost and too often the audience was one jump ahead or the reaction was dulled by familiarity and obviousness. Even here the writers cannot quite live up to our expectations that Groucho will score with every line. But it is necessary to add that anti-climax is a deliberate technique at times. "Three years ago I came to Florida without a nickel in my pocket," he says, reflecting on three years' experience, only to add: "Now I have a nickel in my pocket." Then there is the meaningless observation, "Believe me, you've got to get up early if you want to get out of bed." Such lines carry some risk of suggesting that no strong ending came to mind and when Groucho says there is a written guarantee on every lot "and if these lots don't double their value in a year ...", there is a sense of inspiration failing as he follows his pause with: ". . . I don't know what you can do about it." He solves this in *Duck Soup* when he asks for a loan and offers a personal note for ninety days, adding: "If it isn't paid by then, you can keep the personal note."

James Feibleman makes the observation that "The laconic language of Americans is likewise involved in the humour of these comedians. We have a habit of picking up the telephone in American hotels and saying 'Ice-water in room 412'. Groucho, upon one occasion, is supposed to be desk clerk in a hotel. The telephone rings, and

THE COCOA—NUTS: Party scene. X marks the spot where detective Hennessy's shirt was last seen. Zeppo watches, as does Mrs. Potter rather more doubtfully, while Harpo flirts with Penelope on the other side.

Groucho picks up the receiver. After listening for a moment, he says, 'Ice-water in room 412? Where did you get it?' " [29]

One example of Groucho's changing the meaning of a word with the tone of his voice is interesting as the film's director of photography, George Folsey, recalls it as an instance of improvisation by Groucho. "Let me recall a shot, one of the first we did. We had four cameras on Groucho who was the hotel desk clerk. One of the cameras had a four-inch close-up of Groucho (no rehearsal, mind you) and Groucho rang the bell for the bell-hops. Getting no response, he quickly dived down to the floor and stuck his head out through the opening of his desk. The cameraman didn't know he was going to do this and when he left his picture behind the desk that's the last he ever saw of Groucho. He quickly panned down just as Groucho left the floor and it really was a very amusing but frustrating shot for this poor cameraman." This is the moment in the film (either the cameraman was lucky or it was re-shot because it comes across smoothly) where Groucho, standing in for Zeppo, the real desk clerk, calls "Front!", gets no reply, and drops down to call "Front, front, front!" in the tone of voice used to summon a dog.

Groucho's dialogue is also studded with puns, some obvious, some not so obvious, and many lost because of the density of the other humour. One nicely concealed example lies in some lines delivered to Margaret Dumont. "Your eyes, your eyes, they shine like the pants of my blue serge suit," he tells her (this much a repeat from his dialogue in *I'll Say She Is*) then, as she makes a comment on this, beats his cue with the pun, "That's not a reflection on you, that's on the pants."

* * *

Groucho can handle Margaret Dumont and other people who cross his path, but he has no control over Chico and Harpo. "Gentlemen," says Groucho in *Duck Soup*, pointing to Chico, "Chicolini here may look like an idiot, he may speak like an idiot, but don't let that fool you — he really is an idiot." Groucho speaks with experience. In *The Cocoanuts* he finds Chico is a guest with no money to settle his bill and no concern about it either. He decides to use Chico by getting him to make false bids at the auction to raise prices. Chico manages to grasp the basic idea; but once he's got it he applies it with unyielding tenacity by outbidding everyone else and threatening to gain every lot to Groucho's despair. He is very belligerent about sticking to it despite Groucho's hints and pleas. (This belligerency is only found in *The Cocoanuts;* in later films Chico is always perfectly reasonable, though still quite unshakable.) So firmly embedded is the idea that Groucho has only to announce after the auction that Mrs. Potter is offering a thousand dollars for the return of her necklace for Chico to call out "Two thousand!" At the party, Groucho begins by saying "Ladies and Gentleman", only to have Chico cry

"Two hundred dollars!" It is ironic that the *only* person Groucho tries seriously to reason with and make use of (the others become feeds and stooges) should so elude him.

Chico sports a phoney Italian accent and uses this as an excuse to misunderstand words. He explains to Groucho what he thinks 'auction' means by telling him he came across on the Atlantic Auction and declares that levees on a map means the Jewish neighbourhood (Levys). Chico can't be persuaded that 'a lot' is anything but too much. All his misunderstandings are directed towards a total lack of communication. His puns are generally too far-fetched to be funny in themselves and what is amusing is how absurd they are, for the connection between 'auction' and 'ocean' is barely discernible. The exercising of our minds in linking them together is, in a curious way, half funny and half depressing: the connection is quite unconstructive and stupid, but so far-fetched and unpredictable that it evokes laughter.

In Chico we see stupidity exalted. Worst of all, he can't be made to realise he *is* stupid. It is irritating that he will not be put straight and learn to respect intelligence. But nothing can disturb the complacency with which he lives in this mental twilight. Ignorance is bliss, and his actions suggest that stupidity defeats intelligence every time: something that may not be so very far from the truth. It is difficult enough to speak clearly and reason simply, but even this fails with Chico.

Almost every film has a scene with Chico performing on the piano, usually for an audience. His style can hardly be described but its hallmark is the 'pistol shot technique' by which an extended right index finger stabs at particular notes. His pieces are brash and enjoyable and in music he holds up the tastes of the ignorant man, playing the Beer Barrel Polka and not a Bach Prelude. He displays considerable skill within his chosen style, but his music is in line with the rest of his character. When he sits down to perform for the guests at the party, Mrs. Potter foolishly asks him, "What is the title of your first number?" "Number one!" he announces, holding a finger up in the air to emphasise his non-answer. Whereas Groucho doesn't let himself be pinned down, Chico's evasiveness stems from adhering unshakably to the point.

* * *

In *The Cocoanuts* and most of the later films there is at least one sustained duel of wits between Groucho and Chico, with Groucho gamely fighting to extricate them from the tangle of misunderstanding they have reached. These scenes can be very long, such as that in *The Cocoanuts*, which is also tightly written and one of the best. Almost all of it is done in one five-minute take. It is only by quoting a continuous extract that the flavour of these epic encounters can be

27

THE COCOANUTS: Groucho's party costume amuses Zeppo, Penelope, Harvey Yates, and Mrs. Potter.

properly recalled. Let us take, as our example, Chico's deadly persistence in finding out 'vy a duck'.

Groucho is explaining to Chico his plan for developing the Cocoanut district (from which the film, somewhat loosely, draws its title), and he has a map spread out on a table.

GROUCHO: Now here is a little peninsula, and here is a viaduct leading over to the mainland.

CHICO: Why a duck?

GROUCHO: I'm all right. How are you? I say here is a little peninsula and here is a viaduct leading over to the mainland.

CHICO: All right, why a duck?

GROUCHO: I'm not playing ask me another. I say that's a viaduct.

CHICO: All right, why a duck? Why a duck, why-a no chicken?

GROUCHO: Well, I don't know why-a no chicken. I'm a stranger here myself. All I know is that it's a viaduct. You try to cross over there a chicken and you'll find out vy-a-duck.

CHICO: When I go some place I just —

GROUCHO: It's deep water, that's vy-a-duck. Deep water. Look, look suppose you were out horseback riding and you came to that stream and you wanted to ford over. You couldn't make it. It's too deep.

CHICO: What-a you want with a Ford if you gotta horse?

GROUCHO: Well, I'm sorry the matter ever came up. All I know is that it's a viaduct.

CHICO: I know. All right, I catch on why a horse, why a chicken, why this, why that. I no catch on why a duck.

GROUCHO: I was only fooling. I was only fooling. They're going to build a tunnel there in the morning. Now is that clear to you?

CHICO: Yes, everything except why a duck.

GROUCHO: Well, that's fine. Then we can go ahead with this thing. *After some badinage, quite lost on Chico, about giving him a preferential burial in the local cemetery, Groucho returns to the point and gives Chico directions on how to reach the auction ground.*

GROUCHO: Now you know how to get down there. Now look, now look here, you go down that narrow path there until you come to that little jungle there — you see it? Where those thatched palms are. Then there's a little clearing there, a little clearing with a wire fence around it. You see that wire fence there?

CHICO: All right, why a fence?

GROUCHO: Oh no, we're not going to go through all that again.

* * *

Harpo is a creature of mischief who never hesitates to indulge his every whim and fancy. An apparent simpleton, he is the most complex of the three. He doesn't speak but he is able by whistling, making expressions and miming to express himself with a deeper eloquence not bound by the limitations of words. There is a quality of zest about everything Harpo does; and his whole-hearted enjoyment of life is infectious. He is easily delighted, easily outraged, easily dismayed. He is unpredictable: sometimes he is circumspect, sometimes reckless. There is a childlike air about all his actions; he reduces everything to a game. Although he can be regarded as quite a ruthless figure, he is at heart a boisterous child with a keen sense of mischief who never means any offence. One doesn't except his pursuit of women which is really a game, too, with the fun lying in the chase and perhaps in his naïve ideas of love (watch his playing the great lover with Chico in *At the Circus;* or his indiscriminately kissing everyone goodbye on the boat in *A Night at the Opera,* imitating others through not wanting to be left out).

Petty larceny is a definite instinct with him. Left in charge of the cash register, his first act is to open it and pocket the roll of money he finds. We get an abridged version of his stolen silverware routine with knives dropping out of his sleeve in twos and threes An engaging hint of his past leaks out when he accidentally reveals an old police notice headed 'Silent Red – Wanted by the Police'. (Chico is more deliberately dishonest, planning to pick pockets at the auction and, speaking both for himself and Harpo, letting Groucho know that the empty suitcase they've arrived with will be filled before they leave. Groucho, too, is dishonest in small matters. He picks up the fallen knives that Harpo has dropped and recognises them as his own from the names of the hotels *he* stole them from.)

Harpo's interest in women is most pronounced in *Animal Crackers* and *Monkey Business,* but *The Cocoanuts* is the only film in which Harpo actually and unmistakably catches up with his prey. This occurs at the magnificent moment when Penelope, after constant interruptions by different Marx brothers and the hotel detective, thinks she is alone in her room as Harpo rises from beneath her bed like a pre-historic monster surfacing from the ocean depths. At this point the image diplomatically fades.

She has invited this fate by her earlier encouragement of Harpo as part of a plan to make him the fall-guy for the theft of Mrs. Potter's necklace. She approaches him in a very flirtatious manner and, obviously viewing him as a simpleton, puts on a superior air. First of all she drops a handkerchief beside him. Harpo picks it up with his foot and pockets it. Penelope is forced to ask him if he's seen a handkerchief. Harpo shakes his head. "I thought I dropped one," she says, dripping with *hauteur.* Harpo plays along with this, barely suppressing his sense of mischief, and his face seems to say in a very bored tone, "Oh, did you really?" Penelope tells him it doesn't really matter ". . . because what I'm really interested in is *you.*" Harpo nods and gives her his leg: he has a trick of loading people with it as though it were a detachable object. Penelope starts to lay on the flattery, asking: "Has anyone ever told you that you look like the Prince of Wales?" Faced with this preposterous suggestion, Harpo nods his head to indicate he's heard it all before. "That's funny. I thought it was an original idea of mine." Harpo shakes his head, pooh-poohing that notion. Penelope asks if he knows who she is. Harpo shakes his head negatively. "Do you know my room number?" Harpo nods and his eyes light up wickedly. "Well, I'll be there at eleven o'clock tonight," says Penelope very pronouncedly. She puts her arms around him and he leans on her, smiling and inanely tugging the handkerchief from her breast pocket by his teeth. She walks off in a commanding manner and Harpo follows her, giving a broad imitation of her walk, swinging his hips and giving himself airs. There is about Harpo here a fascinating blend of sickly coyness and mischievous impudence.

Otherwise, Harpo's interest is in young women in general, blondes in particular. They have to be unsuspecting to arouse his interest. One glance at him and they read his intentions and run, encouraging Harpo to give chase. The more women the better to Harpo's way of thinking, which is why, when he discovers that by ringing the bell on the reception counter he can summon a bellhop, he keeps on ringing it. Chico joins in and the bellhops multiply. When a couple of dozen girls have run up, eager to serve, the pair of them dash out and give pursuit as the girls scatter in all directions.

Harpo does not really regard Margaret Dumont as being a woman at all. He delivers iced water to her room, lies out on her bed, and with a broad grin pats the bed cover for her to join him — but this is really to tease her, and sure enough she gets highly indignant. She regards him as some kind of dangerous, unpredictable animal and can be heard during the film uttering with exasperation such lines as, "What's the matter with him *now*?" However, when he has recovered her valuable necklace, she instinctively kisses him. Then, oozing with gratitude, she declares that she must kiss him again. Harpo juts out his chin and lower lip, looking ferocious, and threatens to lay her out if she tries any such thing. He hates the kind of life she represents and this emerges clearly at the party scene which Harpo attends in fancy costume. The style is Spanish and Harpo wears a sash around his trousers, too low down to keep them up, and a wide sombrero hooked under his nose. He swaggers around at first, thoroughly enjoying his masquerade. Later on the speeches start, larded with clichés and weighed down by inexpert hesitations. In disgust, Harpo gets up from the table as each new speaker starts — with his shoulders hunched, arms stiff by his side, face set in a look of fiendish displeasure, teeth gritted together and a cigarette dangling from his mouth. He moves out of frame and later comes back. We discover in time that he has been raiding the punchbowl. He grows quite merry, gives a soft handclap to one of the speakers, and at one time staggers back to his seat to tap his knee, only to have the other leg jerk up in response. Then, by a sort of logical extension, he tries tapping the knee of Penelope, seated next to him. Her leg jerks up into his lap and he strokes it, getting his face slapped. As a whole, Harpo's manner and actions are a purgative for every dull dinner that we spectators have endured, for Harpo doesn't have to conceal his feelings.

His appetite is a third feature of Harpo's character explored in detail by the film. He sits down in the hotel lobby and picks a button off the livery of a page boy standing alongside. He eats it, finds it tasty, and tries another. Later on, he picks up something like a lump of putty in which the pens on the reception counter are stuck, carefully smears it with paste and takes a bite. The watching Groucho is reduced to silence, then proffers a vase of flowers to see what will happen. Harpo carefully selects one and eats it, washing it down with ink from a glass well. Later on, he tries nibbling at a telephone, finds it a little indigestible, carefully swills the ink well and drinks some ink to wash it down. (Director Robert Florey speaks of inventing this bit of business for Harpo, using chocolate and Coca-Cola.[30]) As late as *A Night in Casablanca,* we find Harpo again eating telephones.

The Cocoanuts and *Animal Crackers* also give Harpo a magical ability to spirit objects away from their owners. The hotel detective departs after grilling Chico and Harpo whom he regards with great suspicion (Harpo has flashed him a 'gookie' — the look where his whole face puffs up in a gruesome expression and his lips turn outwards — and leaned on the man so that his motor horn sounds). The detective inadvertently leaves Harpo his badge. At the party he has no sooner arrived to keep an eye on things than he finds that his shirt, the object he should have the least trouble safeguarding, has been whisked off him.

The scene in which Harpo breaks Bob Adams out of jail involves visually the same kind of contradictions and irrelevancies that occur in Groucho's conversation. He arrives encumbered with gardening implements but decides against them as tools for the job. He brings out a mallet and keeps hitting his hand. He produces the key which he has had all along. Bob leaves but Harpo gets locked in. He merely loosens a bar and steps out. Harpo does things the roundabout way for the fun of it, emphasising (as is true of Groucho) that the fun lies in the doing and not in what is done. They live for the moment, without any long-term objectives.

There is the standard opportunity for Harpo to play the harp. Here he is seen creeping rather furtively on to a dais, finding a harp, and playing it, alone and for himself. Chico's pieces are more immediately entertaining and in general the Marxes favour low music. Harpo's higher tastes only come out in private in this film and *Animal Crackers*. Later on, he plays to a crowd but it is always a humble audience. The affectation and ceremony involved in highbrow music like a concert (as in *At the Circus*) or the opera (*A Night at the Opera*) is never associated with Harpo's use of his harp.

Harpo and Chico are partners and have routines of their own in this film. One, which occurs in all five Paramount pictures, is the fight. In this Harpo holds Chico at arm's length and prepares to hit him with a punch from his left fist. Then he moves forward and kicks Chico with his right leg instead. This kind of rowdyism is always breaking out at inopportune moments — when the suspicious hotel detective is watching or when they are in the jail about to release Bob Adams.

Harpo and Chico contrive to get along but at one point Chico declares he is so desperate for money that he would kill for it. He would even kill Harpo. Then he realises that he owes Harpo something for all their years together and so he makes a concession. "No, you're my friend," he declares, "I kill you for nothing." As for Harpo, when Chico vetoes a foolhardy scheme in *Horse Feathers* by saying, "You want to break-a my neck?", he replies by setting about it vigorously. In *Go West*, Groucho inquires if Chico loves his brother Harpo. "No, but I'm used to him," replies Chico. And that just about sums it up.

In *The Cocoanuts*, Harpo and Chico bring off a number of musical parodies of remarkable ingenuity. The detective Hennessy walks up and down contemplating them. They move to each side of him and walk back and forth in step, whistling and turning it into a dance routine until Hennessy breaks it off. Earlier, Harpo is happily playing at the cash register, pressing the keys so that the drawer comes out and thumps his stomach, and the coins vibrate. In no time Chico is banging the bell on top of the nearby cabinet and honking the horn extending from under Harpo's arm as well as singing a tune. All this comes out as part of the Anvil Chorus from *Il Trovatore*, the very opera they turn upside down in *A Night at the Opera* (written also by Kaufman and Ryskind which perhaps explains the parallel). Then Harpo annoys Harvey Yates and Penelope so much that he drags her away labelling Harpo a "bum". Harpo savours the word and mouths it to himself. Chico repeats it thoughtfully aloud and his "bum ... bum ... bum ..." seems to be the beating of a drum. They become soldiers, Harpo starts whistling, Groucho joins on the end 'playing' his cigar as a mouth organ and with a handkerchief draped over his forehead, and the three of them march off screen to the tune of 'Yankee Doodle Dandy'. Lastly, at the party, Harpo blows a smoke bubble out of his mouth and lets it break in Groucho's face. "Tis a breath of old Ireland!" exclaims Groucho in an Irish accent and all four Marx Brothers perform an Irish jig. These moments are suddenly and fully developed on the thinnest pretext. They are evidence of a hidden *rapport* between the characters. No other film has much of this, though the climax to *Duck Soup* is partly a medley of musical numbers.

Groucho is no match for either of his brothers. He tries hard to deal with Chico but is defeated by Chico's bottomless stupidity. With Harpo he doesn't attempt to argue. After a couple of short lessons from the mute redhead, he shows a healthy respect tinged with fascination. As he puts it when his dinner speech drives Harpo away with that ghastly expression on his countenance: "The one I've got rid of is worth three ordinary ones."

The first lesson comes when he goes forward to shake Harpo's hand as the latter walks into the hotel. Harpo's own hand goes up so that Groucho's hand slaps against it and Harpo can slap his face in return. They try again but Harpo has his bulb horn concealed in his hand, it sounds, and Groucho — displaying a trait of cowardice widely seen in these films — rushes behind the counter to safety.

He does make one small effort to deter Harpo from using the reception desk pens as darts to fling at the wall, but then concedes and encourages him. It suddenly becomes a fairground sideshow as Groucho starts calling "This way, folks! Three shots for ...", a bell rings, and he hands Harpo a cigar.

Harpo's strange appetite fascinates him, so much so that he lapses into a rare silence. When Harpo moves over to the pigeon holes and starts tearing up the letters, Groucho is compelled to help him along by handing some to him and apologising for the absence of the afternoon post.

*   *   *

This, then, is the character of the Marxes as established by their first film and largely maintained afterwards.

There are not many scenes where all the Marx Brothers come together and some of these have, a little misleadingly, been regarded from the point of view of each brother and not as a whole. Most of Zeppo's scenes are with Groucho at the reception desk, but all four take part in the musical burlesque of *Carmen*, 'The Tale of a Shirt', after Harpo has gone to work on Hennessy. Groucho, Chico and Harpo notably work on each other at their first meeting in the hotel lobby; in the accelerated bedroom farce of Harpo and Chico's rendezvous with Penelope while Groucho and the detective are visiting Mrs. Potter in the next room; and as guests at the dinner party.

What also serves to unite the Marx brothers is a concern for Polly and Bob, the hero and heroine. Groucho likes Polly enough to give her a genial introduction to a song and sit back without making a single comment. He thinks of breaking Bob out of jail when Polly is betrothed to Harvey Yates, and despatches Harpo and Chico to do it. Harpo is so moved at seeing her left alone on the auction ground, sobbing as Bob is taken to jail, that he comes up and offers her a lollipop and a shoulder to cry on. There is no call for sympathy by Harpo and his face is completely expressionless — but it is a sentimental gesture quite out of keeping with anything done in the other Paramount films.

The final impression the film is meant to leave is that the Marxes have themselves been stooges — for the romance. They are shown waving inanely at the camera before being deprived of the closing shot. One feels they ought to have advanced and split the screen wide open, or thrown cocoanuts at Bob and Polly as they throw apples at Margaret Dumont to end *Duck Soup*.

4. Animal Crackers (1930)

With *Duck Soup, Animal Crackers* is probably the best known of the early Marx films. More of Groucho's quips seem to have reached common currency from it than from any other film and Captain Spaulding is probably the first part that people would associate with him. However, *Animal Crackers* cannot be ranked as high as *The Cocoanuts*. The Marxes are able to figure quite as memorably at moments but there are long patches where Groucho's dialogue is not so brilliant while the Groucho-Chico scenes become rather ponderous. It is a lengthy film with much more of the Marx Brothers than its predecessor, for the romantic couple here have been cut back to one song and only one real scene to themselves while the plot is openly farcical and scarcely impedes the film at all. Taking only the Marx scenes in *The Cocoanuts*, these seem more entertaining and more satisfying than the general level reached by the team with the increased exposure of *Animal Crackers*. This is odd because Kaufman and Ryskind are again the writers (Kalmar and Ruby only did the music and lyrics here, though they were also scriptwriters on *Horse Feathers* and *Duck Soup*).

Speaking cinematically, there is little advance on *The Cocoanuts*. Again filmed on the Astoria sound stages, it boasts many perfor-

ANIMAL CRACKERS: Groucho, as Captain Spaulding, is playing up to Margaret Dumont as Mrs. Rittenhouse (N.B. in the film itself Groucho rolls up his trouser leg but kneels on the other knee).

mances that are hopelessly theatrical — Margaret Dumont is still working very hard switching expressions to order. And when the tin sheets are rattled to simulate thunder, the illusion of watching a stage is complete.

The setting is Rittenhouse Manor on Long Island, the occasion a party given by Mrs. Rittenhouse (who is, of course, Margaret Dumont). She hopes to reap the social honours of the season and has two special treats lined up for her guests. The first is the unveiling of a Beaugard painting just acquired in Europe by the celebrated art critic and collector, Roscoe W. Chandler, who is going to introduce the work. The second is the appearance of the celebrated Captain Jeffrey T. Spaulding direct from an expedition into the jungle.

As in the party scene of *The Cocoanuts*, Zeppo precedes Groucho. In fact, as Horatio W. Jamison, the Captain's field secretary, he is the first Marx Brother on screen and this helps to give him some prominence. He enters into the 'Hooray for Captain Spaulding' number that the excited guests have started, singing Groucho's conditions for attending. Then Groucho as the Captain is borne in by four African natives in a chair, ostensibly all the way from Africa. This touch, taken with his boots, riding pants and pith helmet, is the only one to suggest Groucho has had any actual experience of Africa and it is so excessively authentic that one could almost see him as a fraud who had hired the costume and bearers from a theatrical agency. He dismisses their bill for transporting him from Africa (varied, but invariably amusing, are the means he adopts to evade paying charges through the Marx films). Mrs. Rittenhouse comes forward to greet him while he is browbeating the leading native only to be rudely waved back with the remark, "I'll deal with you later!" Then follows the rest of the number. While the chorus are singing, Groucho throws himself about and leaps around in a madly athletic dance. Part of the time he is hopping around on one leg, rotating the other like a corkscrew (as he does again during the *Horse Feathers* opening number), and he also simulates trudging through the jungle. This over, Groucho eyes the palatial residence and starts telling Mrs. Rittenhouse what she should do with it to improve business, naturally assuming that it is a commercial enterprise, and goes on to try and sell her an insurance policy with a line of sales talk that casts the usual aspersions on her age and breeding: "I want to tell you, madam, that with this insurance policy you're provided for your little ones and for your old age, which will be here in a couple of weeks now if I'm any judge of horse flesh."

Nothing Groucho says, here or in his later speech about his African trip, does anything to substantiate his reputation as a fearless explorer, but then nothing can shake the faith of these society people in him, even when he faints at the sight of a caterpillar. He is prized not for his exploits but simply as a celebrity whose every foible must

ANIMAL CRACKERS: Groucho, as Captain Spaulding, makes
his grand entrance.

be excused or overlooked if he is to stay. It is Mrs. Rittenhouse
who builds him up by telling everyone how brave he is and Groucho
who pours scorn on her words. "Sez you" he sneers, lacking the least
gratitude for her efforts on his behalf. When he makes love to Mrs.
Rittenhouse and another guest, Mrs. Whitehead, simultaneously and
then goes off with some younger female guests leaving them high and
dry, they merely remark "The Captain's so amusing!" "Isn't he
charming!" They are quite unable, or rather, unwilling, to see through
their own image of him.

Mrs. Rittenhouse is much less stuffy than Mrs. Potter. In fact, she
is probably the nicest *grande dame* portrayed by Margaret Dumont. She is rather tickled by the duel in puns, quoted later, that
Groucho and Chico put on. She is a little concerned about her daugh·
ter Arabella's interest in a man of no social position, a would-be artist called John Parker, but seems genuinely disturbed when it looks
as though he is the one who has removed her precious Beaugard
painting. When Groucho reaches the point of declaring, in his African
reminiscences, "We took some pictures of the native girls but they
weren't developed. But we're going back in a couple of weeks
and...!", she discreetly concludes the lecture, showing that she is a
woman of tact as well as propriety. Some of her ideas are a bit old-
fashioned, of course. "Marriage is a very noble institution!" she
spouts and Groucho whinnies in contempt. (To him "It was put over
on the American people while our boys were over there!" — just the

kind of emotional, colourful phrase we might find in a political speech, but spoken in this wildly inappropriate context its scope for mis-use becomes very apparent.)

Overall, Mrs. Rittenhouse is rather sympathetic and quite undeserving of the brutal mishandling she receives from Harpo. She is also on the receiving end of some more romantic patter from Groucho. He finds her alone, yoo-hooing her and miaowing, then scolding her sharply for taking a little simple pleasure in acting the innocent with him. He then becomes embarrassed and struggles to unburden his heart. "Mrs. Rittenhouse, ever since I've met you I've swept you off my feet. Something has been throbbing within me — oh, it's been beating like the incessant tom-tom in the primitive jungle. There's something I must ask you. Would you wash out a pair of socks for me?" She is rather surprised but Groucho reassures her simply by adding: "It's just my way of telling you that I love you, that's all."

Apart from Arabella, the other posh figures are all shown to be phonies or frauds, quite without the dignity they assume. Roscoe W. Chandler is really a fish-peddler from Czechoslovakia called Abe Cabiddle; Hives, the mannered butler, has a criminal record and is disloyal to his employer; Mrs. Whitehead and her daughter make an unbearably snooty pair, trying jealously to sabotage Mrs. Rittenhouse's arrangements. Arabella Rittenhouse is a bit of a snob herself, horrified to learn that her mother has invited a fish peddler into the house and willing to urge John Parker to marry her and live off mother's expense account. But she is also rather engaging thanks to Lillian Roth's bubbling personality and she is willing to marry below her station as well as sharing none of Mrs. Whitehead's concern about John Parker's family. In general, the kind of society debunked by the Marx brothers is shown to be worth very little. As a complete contrast, the Marxes act as they feel, not caring in the least what others think.

Chandler is a pompous oaf who automatically roars with laughter as Groucho says, "Have you heard the one about the two Irishmen?", though Groucho doesn't go on to tell him the joke. Chandler laughs to show how sociable he is, just as in *The Cocoanuts* the

ANIMAL CRACKERS: An "indecently clad" Harpo goes on a shooting rampage. Hives, the butler with shattered champagne bottle, looks alarmed.

guests all laugh in polite anticipation of the same joke only to find Groucho has forgotten it, making their response quite pointless. We also see Chandler's readiness to bore anyone when Groucho asks his opinion of art and he launches into a long monologue that Groucho hastily cuts short.

Two branches of the arts are directly satirised in *Animal Crackers*. The famous Beaugard painting, along with two imitations (one painted by Mrs. Whitehead's daughter, the other by John Parker), becomes creased and crumpled as it travels around and is even slept in by Harpo. Nobody worries about little things like this or the way Chandler clutches at the canvas at the end in inspecting it: the important point is that the painting is there.

Secondly, Groucho delivers a broadside at the theatre, especially the area dominated by Eugene O'Neill who also undergoes a further gibe or two in *Horse Feathers*. But there is nothing vindictive about this, or about any of the Marx comedy. Groucho first moves into his sham theatricals during a scene with Mrs. Rittenhouse and Mrs. Whitehead by separating himself from himself. One Groucho steps aside and comments on the other. "He shot her a glance," says Groucho, then shooting his eyes sideways to become his other self. "And a smile played around his lips," he adds, then fluttering his lips. The two women, he declares, between them add up to the ideal woman. This merging of them and splitting of himself is one of the many fleeting attacks on the individual's identity that occur throughout the Marx *oeuvre*.

He then delivers three O'Neill-like soliloquies by stepping forward, ending them by shooting his eyes upwards and stepping back. In one he refers to the pair of women as a couple of baboons, in another he assumes a heavy, introspective melancholy ("The Gods look down and laugh") that mocks the portentousness of this kind of theatre, and concludes with the much quoted aphorism, "How much better it would be for the children if the parents had to eat the spinach." Oddly enough, there is a lot of sense in this observation and the amusement lies really in the sympathetic recall of childhood restrictions. He then spells out a future with Margaret Dumont: "You could live with your folks and I — I could live with *your* folks", his emphasis of the word 'your' implying a contrast that isn't in the words. This line prompts a third soliloquy that is worth quoting in all its barnacled language and delightful crude anticlimax. Groucho says it in a mock-solemn, echoing intonation: "Living with your folks. Living with your folks. The beginning of the end. Drab dead yesterdays shutting out beautiful tomorrows. Hideous, stumbling footsteps creaking along the misty corridors of time. And in those corridors I see figures ... [his voice grows deeper and clouded] ... strange figures ... weird figures ... [then back to normal voice:] ... Steel 186, Anaconda 74, American Cane 138 ..."

Here again he throws out the 'elevated thought' and brings in some lowbrow, topical, basely commercial reference, just as Mrs. Rittenhouse's lavishly appointed home is likened to a cheap hotel. Similarly, in a conversation with Chandler, Groucho seizes on the familiar but meaningless phrase "art is art" as part of a brilliant chain of illogical argument so quickly delivered that it is impossible to unravel it, giving it a richly ludicrous, irresistibly funny quality. He is suggesting where Chandler might build an Opera House. "Why don't you put it in the reservoir and get the whole thing over with? Of course, that might interfere with the water supply. But after all we must remember that art is art. Still, on the other hand, water is water, isn't it, and east is east and west is west and if you take cranberries and stew them like apple sauce they taste much more like prunes than rhubarb does. Now, er — now you tell me what you know." As in his lecture on alligator pears in *The Cocoanuts*, Groucho skilfully ends by throwing the ball back into the other court: Chandler has to pick up the conversation.

Another asinine remark of Chandler's — "The nickel today is not worth what it used to be ten years ago" — is sufficient for Groucho to launch into a finely nonsensical solution that knowingly appeals for thrift and progressive thinking. "I'll go further than that," he declares to Chandler, "I'll get off at the depot. The nickel today is not what it was *fifteen* years ago. Do you know what this country needs today? A seven cent nickel. Yes sirree, we've been using the

ANIMAL CRACKERS: Groucho is annoyed at the quibbling of his secretary Zeppo while Mrs. Rittenhouse looks alarmed at his display of temperament in this dictation scene.

five cent nickel in this country since 1492 and that's pretty near a hundred years daylight saving. Now why not give the seven cent nickel a chance? If that works out, next year we could have an eight-cent nickel. Think what that would mean. You could go to a news-stand, buy a three cent newspaper and get the same nickel back again. One nickel carefully used would last a family a lifetime!"

In Groucho's conversation with Chandler, there is at the start the usual rigmarole about introductions with Groucho repeatedly intro-ducing himself and Chandler doing likewise. But this insistence on their separate identities eventually leads to the pair being so con-fused that Groucho turns to the audience (i.e. to camera) and asks to see a programme to find out who he is. This is rather forced, as there are only two of them to generate the confusion, and is acted out as genuine confusion on Groucho's part (unlike, say, the proliferation of Steinbergs being introduced to one another as a delaying gambit in, *A Day at the Races;* or the introduction of Gottlieb to Mrs. Claypool in *A Night at the Opera* where Groucho is playing with them). Throughout *Animal Crackers,* Groucho becomes a man who automa-tically creates such muddles. He introduces himself to a second detec-tive called Hennessy (the first was the hotel dick in *The Cocoanuts*) as "Captain Scotland of Spaulding Yard". He is proud of his own record in investigating cases: once he stepped in they were never solved. The Beaugard painting disappears, Groucho declares, "Let's bring some light to this case", and the lights immediately go out. This lack of command is a new aspect of Groucho's character and one that is not seen again. It is rather wearisome compared to Groucho's usual control over words and people.

On the other hand, there are examples of Groucho's misplacing words deliberately and so cunningly that in most places they are scarcely, if at all, noticeable. "Don't you remember Mrs. Beaugard lost a valuable Rittenhouse oil painting worth one hundred thousand dollars?" asks Groucho and because the words are familiar and we know roughly what is being said the misplacement of words is apt to pass us by. That is perhaps a more obvious one but what about Groucho asking Mrs. Potter, "Do you know property values have increased 1929 since 1000%?" or telling Bob Adams "What's the use of worrying? You're gone today and here tomorrow" in *The Cocoa-nuts?* They suggest, like so much of the Marx Brothers work, how tricky a means language is for communicating what we have to say. It is much more satisfying when we can believe Groucho does it deliberately or is indifferent to his mistakes, for when he tries to sort out the confusion he puts himself in the same class as the rest of us. Groucho's rise above such muddle, along with his attack on all social conventions, is heroic, and we identify with him perhaps as much as we do with more conventional screen heroes. Certainly the men in an audience relish Groucho's rudeness towards Margaret Dumont.

ANIMAL CRACKERS: Groucho and Chico examine the formerly missing painting as Arabella Rittenhouse (Lillian Roth) and John Parker (Hal Thompson) listen attentively.

Zeppo is used as a foil in the letter scene. Groucho's letter, dictated to Zeppo as his secretary, is filled with the jargon of business correspondence, the *to wits* and *ipso factos*, to the exclusion of any content. He finishes off with "Hoping this finds you" and Zeppo raises an objection, wanting to know *where* it finds him. This would seem to be the first point to have struck Zeppo as worth querying but in fact he has found the whole body of the letter unimportant and left it out. He has also omitted a Hungerdunger from the law firm of Hungerdunger, Hungerdunger, Hungerdunger, Hungerdunger and MacCormick. "You've left out the main one, too," exclaims Groucho, making an impossible differentiation between the Hungerdungers he has named. This is the logical corollary of Groucho's attacks on the individual's identity. When there is no particular individual capable of being recognised, Groucho insists on finding one, the main Hungerdunger.

But, as in this letter scene, much of Groucho's dialogue is rather flat and makes no real impression. "Well, all the jokes can't be good," he says to the audience. Again he has many puns and at least a couple of them are ingenious. "Why, that's bigamy!" declares Mrs. Rittenhouse when Groucho proposes to her and Mrs. Whitehead at the same time. "And it's bigamy, too!" replies Groucho. Perhaps it is symptomatic of the decline of the pun that we are more alert to them and don't need Groucho to spell it out by adding, "It's big of all of us." An inane form of humour seems to appear and cause a groan when Groucho dictates the word 'fragilly' to Zeppo; but then he outwits us by telling Zeppo to consult the dictionary under 'fragile', thereby distinguishing it from the word we thought he intended to say. This kind of extra twist that undermines a situation as it stands is a common feature of the Marxes' work (cf. Harpo's jail scene in *The Cocoanuts*).

* * *

Chico is one of the musicians employed to play for Mrs. Rittenhouse. He arrives by the front entrance instead of the back and, as soon as he is introduced to the lady of the house, inquires: "Where's the dining room?" Food is as much an obsessive preoccupation with Chico as it is with Harpo: the appetites of the Marxes are very fundamental — food, drink, money, music and games about sum it up. When Groucho was showing Chico on the map Cocoanut Manor, Cocoanut Heights, Cocoanut Junction, etc., during *The Cocoanuts* Chico's only query was: "Where you got coconut custard?" In *Monkey Business* Groucho talks of the shortcut taken by Christopher Columbus and Chico knows all about a shortcut: strawberry shortcut (i.e. shortcake).

For Mrs. Rittenhouse, Chico elaborates a scale of fees by which he is paid more for rehearsing than playing and most for not playing at all. At the concert he has a chance to play and performs 'Sugartime', monotonously repeating part of it as if it were some dull piano exercise. It transpires that he's forgotten how it finishes, and he remarks ominously that he once kept it up for three whole days. Here, as in the bidding of *The Cocoanuts*, Chico is clinging tenaciously to one idea: finishing the number. How rigidly his mind is attuned to certain ways is also revealed when Arabella asks him to substitute her boy friend's copy of the Beaugard for the real thing. She assures him that it isn't stealing. In that case he won't do it. Chico is only interested in dishonesty.

* * *

Groucho starts querying Chico's identity on the latter's arrival in the film's earliest example of confusion-of-identity. "Hey," concludes Chico laughing, "He thinks I look alike." Groucho adds the customary crack at Chico's expense, "Well, if you do, it's a tough break for both of you." He is soon asking Chico, "How much would you want to run into an open manhole?" (cf. ". . . stand at the wrong end of a shooting gallery?" in *Horse Feathers* and other such lines). "Just the cover charge!" replies Chico brightly, laughing at his own pun (which is unusual). "Well, drop in some time," suggests Groucho. "Sewer!" says Chico (i.e. sure). "Well, we cleaned that up pretty well," concludes Groucho, and with this comment one is apt to agree. It is again in the quiz-like spirit of many Marx conversations, one trying to outdo the other. The real Groucho-Chico confrontation comes late in the film when it is obviously near its conclusion. This is where the pair of them are lethargically discussing the missing Beaugard and how to locate the thief. Chico has the idea of asking everyone in the house if they stole it. Groucho offers a practical objection. It has nothing to do with whether the thief would own up if asked. Instead it is: "Suppose nobody in the house took the painting?" Chico takes a short, logical step forward: "Go to the house next door." Groucho counters that: "Suppose there isn't any house next door?" Chico thinks past this objection, but his mind doesn't range back to the basic objective. "Then, of course, we gotta build one," he declares. Groucho's interest is suddenly awakened and the pair set about drawing up detailed plans for this entirely irrelevant house. A maid's room is laid out between Chico's and Groucho's room and sounds as though it will be as busy as Penelope's bedroom in *The Cocoanuts* or Connie Bailey's apartment in *Horse Feathers*. When Groucho brings up the matter of the stolen painting again, Chico has completely forgotten about it (like the ending of 'Sugartime'). But this scene is too long and static for so late a place in the film, and it tends to drag a little.

* * *

Chico and Harpo evidently know each other. While Chico is trying to work out where he has seen Chandler before (and Chandler is denying any previous acquaintance with Chico), Harpo is chasing a blonde down and up some steps in the background. Chico calls

ANIMAL CRACKERS: Harpo and Chico examine a check extracted from Roscoe W. Chandler (Louis Sorin) as a bribe to keep his background quiet.

Harpo over to see if he knows Chandler, then recalls that he's Abie the Fish Peddler from Czechoslovakia. He denies it vehemently and is upended in a search for an identifying birthmark. They find the large black mark on the back of Chandler's arm. Chico asks him how he came to be Chandler and there is an interesting comeback: "Say, how did you come to be an Italian?" "Never mind, whose confession is this?" retorts Chico but it is nice to have him exposed as the fake we always knew he was. Chandler tries to bribe them to keep his background quiet. Harpo wrings his hands in anticipatory glee at the money he will get. Chandler produces a roll of bills which Chico rejects as insufficient. In pocketing it, Chandler unknowingly places it in Harpo's trousers just as Harpo collected the jailer's key to rescue Bob Adams in *The Cocoanuts*. Harpo also puts his magical ability to work again so that Chandler's tie and handkerchief vanish. When he eventually gets away, he has left Chico with his tie and Harpo with — his birthmark! The very thing that gave Chandler his old identity has been taken by Harpo in a concrete, if extreme, suggestion of the precariousness of identity. However, this magical talent is one that Harpo desists from using in later films.

Chico and Harpo also get to work on their host. Harpo keeps handing Mrs. Rittenhouse his leg. When rebuked, he stands to attention, grinning away as he feigns obedience. Chico hands her his leg and soon after Harpo is slapping her thigh so that her leg jerks up. She decides, with Mrs. Whitehead, to sit down but finds that Harpo has arrived beneath her as she does so. After some swinging of Harpo's leg on to Mrs. Whitehead's lap, Harpo swings it in the opposite direction on to Chico's lap and the pair progressively entwine themselves as in *The Cocoanuts*. Mrs. Rittenhouse has meanwhile walked away. Harpo dashes after her, apparently with the intention of wrapping himself around her as he has just done with Chico. She breaks free from his grasp, he swings a punch at her and falls over. While she and Mrs. Whitehead are discussing this, they are quite unaware (unlike the audience) that trouble is brewing. Chico is busily reviving Harpo by tickling his tummy and giving him his instructions for Round Two. From somewhere a bell rings and Harpo comes out fighting, towards the quite unsuspecting figure of Margaret Dumont as Mrs. Rittenhouse. This produces the most barbaric image found in any Marx film. He grabs her and punches her repeatedly in the stomach so that she rises into the air. We can laugh at this image as (1) the unpardonable, anarchic image of a dignified lady being beaten up; (2) as a visual metaphor, society becoming a punchbag for the Marx Brothers. In the latter respect, it is like Groucho grappling with Margaret Dumont in *The Cocoanuts* and putting up his fists, only here Harpo actually wades into her. We couldn't ordinarily enjoy such a sight but we can here because of the particular characters involved and because, while Harpo's fero-

ANIMAL CRACKERS: Mrs. Rittenhouse in not amused by
Harpo's behavior in the card game. Chico is. Mrs. Whitehead
(Margaret Irving) looks uncertain.

cious build-up lets us imagine he is really going to hurt her, the limp
way she actually rises in the air reassures us that Harpo is pulling
his punches and lifting her.

Naturally, Mrs. Rittenhouse (we only think of her as Margaret
Dumont in extreme moments apart from her scenes with Groucho)
suffers no bad after-effects from this 'sport' and the four of them
are able to sit down and play cards. As a sign that he expects an
honest game, Harpo carefully rolls up his sleeves and lays a black-
jack on the table. Mrs. Rittenhouse reaches out a hand in telling him
to put it away, using exactly the tone of voice aunts employ in re-
buking a child. Harpo picks up the offending object and whacks at
her outstretched hand, contriving to actually hit his own hand so
that he can pretend to have hurt it. (This is a game he always enjoys:
in opening the cell in *The Cocoanuts*, he aimed a mallet at the lock
but hit his hand, moved the hand further away and then hit it again,
all for the fun of it as he had the key all the time.) He holds out his
'injured' hand towards Mrs. Whitehead for her to kiss and make well,
then threatens to hit her if she does, putting on the same sour expression he gave Harvey Yates in the hotel lobby during *The Cocoanuts*.

His dramatic demand for honest play proves to be a blind as he
indulges in the most blatant cheating, knowing that the two ladies
are not too certain of the game, won't be expecting in polite society
such outrageously obvious cheating, and will hesitate to create a
fuss. Mrs. Rittenhouse is a little surprised when two aces of spades

46

turn up in cutting for partners. Harpo shuffles the cards by letting the edges flick through his fingers without changing their order at all. He is made to cut but merely puts the two piles together as they were before. He deals one-handedly, wetting the thumb of his other hand but not using it to separate the cards. He shows Chico each card to see if he wants it, the ladies being too busy sorting their cards to notice. Harpo's methods are not the sophisticated ones of the professional cardsharp but have the directness and simplicity we expect from him. There is no elaborate calculation: apart from the rigged deck, the cheating is done on the spur of the moment.

When Chico doesn't fancy a particular card, Harpo throws it away. (Perversely, he later stops to retrieve a card which falls on the floor and has just gone out of play.) He then deals Mrs. Rittenhouse four bad cards in a row and proceeds to demonstrate how little difference it makes anyway (whatever she is dealt, Harpo will win) by swopping her cards for his.

Later, Chico does consent to put up the Beaugard imitation for Arabella and recruits Harpo to help him. As it is dark when they steal into the library, Chico asks for the "flesh". Harpo pinches his face. That's not it. Harpo goes on to produce a spray can of Flit, a fish, a flute, a flush of cards, etc., before realising Chico wants a flash or flashlight. Thereupon Harpo switches on a torch to look for the flashlight. Harpo always enjoys misunderstanding demands: asked for his passport in *Monkey Business*, he produces a pasteboard and washboard before finding the passport. Of course, this confusion with Chico is quite ridiculous because he is deliberately mispronouncing the word: Chico's fake Italian accent makes difficulties even for himself.

ANIMAL CRACKERS: Harpo and Chico embark on their fight routine in the concert scene.

At the concert, Harpo is also unamused by Chico's efforts on the piano. His face takes on that displeased expression and he starts clanging together a couple of horseshoes. Immediately Chico responds on the piano and the pair of them beat out part of the Anvil Chorus as they did in a different way during *The Cocoanuts*.

* * *

ANIMAL CRACKERS: Harpo arrives at the start of the film and makes a "gookie" watched by Hives, footmen, and guests.

Harpo is the last to make a grand entrance at the start of the film. He is announced as "The Professor" but a professor of what — except, perhaps, blonde-chasing — is never made apparent. He is obviously an uninvited guest crashing the party. He is dressed for the occasion in an evening cloak beneath which can be glimpsed a silk shirt and bow tie. On his head he wears a top hat, which is not battered as in later films, covering his wig (here and in subsequent films a lighter colour than it was in *The Cocoanuts*). He carries a cane to complete the picture of the well-dressed gentleman and strides down the steps towards Mrs. Rittenhouse and her guests in a nonchalant manner with an odd, fixed grin on his face. (Here, and for the entrances of the others, Harry Ruby's ingenious musical accompaniment greatly enhances the effect.) Harpo's head seems a

48

little loosely fitted to his body and its swaying motions are picked up by the music.

Harpo has gained everyone's attention and Hives, the butler, steps up to take his cloak. Away it comes leaving him standing there in vest and pants. The guests are all horrified. This is another key image. Again the artificial standards of society are attacked. Harpo is reasonably attired for an athletics track but in this context he is positively indecent. Yet this indecency is really in the mind of the beholder.

A couple of Harpo's favourite routines emerge before the guests are scattered by his use of a rifle. Shaking Mrs. Rittenhouse's hand, he has the motor horn concealed as he did for greeting Groucho in *The Cocoanuts*. He also lets out smoke bubbles that rise and break. "You haven't got chocolate, have you?" inquires the watching Groucho, distinctly intrigued. Harpo smiles and blows out a black bubble. As Chico so aptly remarks: "He's got everything."

At the end of the film he is shaking hands with a police inspector who is solemnly warning him that he must live a better life in future (he has produced the missing Beaugard and almost been arrested). A few knives drop to the floor. Harpo quickly glances upwards causing the inspector to do likewise and have his attention diverted. But as the lecture continues and Harpo's hand is steadily shaken, the knives keep dropping out of his other sleeve. Harpo's face is still and almost expressionless — just slightly tinged with apprehension. Chico is looking on with anticipatory enjoyment; Groucho also watches with pleasure. Here they step out of character and, without detracting from the film, show that this is a routine they have seen many times before. We have, too, in *The Cocoanuts* on a less elaborate scale; and for us, as well as for Harpo's brothers, it is an enjoyable ritual to be played out in its own time to an inevitable conclusion. "This may go on for years," Groucho tells us from experience, knowing the fantastic capacity of Harpo's raincoat. "I can't understand what's delaying that coffee pot," he comments in the voice of the connoisseur and immediately afterwards it obligingly tumbles out.

Harpo is not upset by this involuntary confession of his thieving. But during *Animal Crackers* there is the curious moment when he is on the loose with a rifle, taking potshots at everything. Among his targets is a statue of two wrestlers. They suddenly come to life and shoot back at him. Harpo suffers a slight reverse, being taken aback by this. It raises a laugh from audiences but is contrary to the whole spirit of Harpo's character, that he is never put out by anything. In as much as this is surrealistic and the statue is from classical Greek art (Harpo's character is in some ways linked to this period and its mythology). Harpo's command over the contemporary world is not upset, but all the same it doesn't come across as being right.

It is the world of the Marx Brothers that is sane and orderly, and we who are out of step. Mrs. Whitehead sets out to engage Harpo's attention while Hives creeps up from behind to smother Harpo with ether and gain the painting which he has in his possession. She tries the same kind of condescending flattery that Penelope used in *The Cocoanuts*, telling him that she likes little boys like him. Does he perhaps like anyone: is there someone precious in his life? Harpo nods and produces a photograph of the loved one. It shows a horse. Mrs. Whitehead giggles with amusement while Harpo looks baffled and indicates that *she* must be quite mad.

The same ether that temporarily subdues Harpo comes to his aid at the moment he is about to be arrested for the stolen property he has dropped. He sprays the ether, which he has loaded into a Flit can, over the inspector and then systematically puts down all the guests. Groucho goes under, leaving a recalcitrant foot in the air to be sprayed down by Harpo. Chico, trying to see his partner safely away, gets a whiff and collapses. Then Harpo himself, the mighty warrior who has won a bloodless victory and entirely triumphed over the enemy, surveys the stage full of bodies, spies the blonde he has been chasing at intervals during the film, and sprays himself to sleep beside her. The succession of fleeting images comes to an end as the final title appears on the screen after a dissolve into perfect peace. There is a Shakespearian magic and power about it. One would not be wrong to think of Prospero declaring: "We are such stuff as dreams are made on; and our little life is rounded with a sleep." We, too, have seen a vision on baseless fabric, an insubstantial pageant that has dissolved away but not without making its lasting impression.

ANIMAL CRACKERS: Harpo threatens to break the arm of Mrs. Whitehead when she engages him in conversation.

5. Monkey Business (1931)

The team's first screen original was made in Hollywood under the direction of Norman McLeod. It was also the first of the only two Marx Brothers' films to bear the name of S. J. Perelman, who recently published an article about how he came to work on the film.[16] His collaborator on the screenplay was Will B. Johnstone (who had scripted *I'll Say She Is*, the Marxes' first success on Broadway) and Arthur Sheekman came in later to add to the script. Perelman went on to work at the next script, *Horse Feathers*, and is commonly regarded as having had a great influence on the team. We can consider how justified this is after looking at *Monkey Business* and before dealing with *Horse Feathers*.

* * *

All four of the Marxes are stowaways on an ocean liner. It is the

MONKEY BUSINESS: Life in a kippered herring barrel. The four stowaways (Harpo, Zeppo, Chico, and Groucho) relax after singing 'Sweet Adeline'.

only film in which Groucho lacks some kind of position. He is merely a stowaway like his brothers whereas, when the same sort of situation arises in *A Night at the Opera*, Groucho is travelling, however uncomfortably, as a legitimate passenger on the boat through his connection with Margaret Dumont, leaving Chico and Harpo (taking with them the romantic lead) to be the stowaways in his luggage.

Here, then, Groucho becomes an outsider like his brothers, to be chased around the deck and regarded as odd by the normal characters. At times Groucho is distinctly diminished. There is at least an improvement on his character in *Animal Crackers* when he fainted at the sight of a caterpillar on his lapel: he now asserts himself as a man who has licked his way *from* wild caterpillars. But the old trait of cowardice reappears when he first hears the name of the notorious gangster Joe Helton, while he and Zeppo are so uncomfortable about the pistols they are given to use on Helton that they quickly drop them in the nearest bucket of water. Even worse is the moment at the party when Helton and some of the guests laugh at Groucho's imitation of a bowlegged Texan. Their laughter has a ring of superiority; perplexed shrugs would be more in order. But on the whole Groucho manages to assert himself splendidly, and the film does have the pleasing effect of uniting the four brothers from the start as occupants of four barrels marked 'Kippered Herring' in the hold of a ship. They sing 'Sweet Adeline' (in song — with Harpo mouthing enthusiastically — is one of the strongest ways the Marxes show their *rapport* with one another), and when their barrels are hoisted in a search of the hold they are displayed calmly carrying on with their different activities as though they had every right in the world to be there: Groucho whisking an egg, Zeppo pouring tea, Chico and Harpo with coffee pots. Clearly the barrels have all modern conveniences. At a shout from the First Officer, the foursome look up simultaneously and regard him fixedly to know the meaning of this disturbance. Then after this steady pause, the four of them break off and run, still acting in unison. During the chase, the four run down some steps on one side of a decorative pool. Chico and Zeppo run round and up the other side. Groucho is about to follow until restrained by Harpo.

MONKEY BUSINESS: The "winsome foursome" pause during the chase to improvise on saxes.

The pair wait in a clear expression of family solidarity for Chico and Zeppo to come down again before they move off together. They run on to an orchestra dais and pick up abandoned instruments, going straight into a lively number, Chico on piano, the other three swaggering up and down playing saxophones, the four stamping their feet together at the end, a wave of applause breaking out as they resume their role in the chase.

However, it is not long before they have split up and are involved in separate episodes of their own.

*   *   *

Backed by faint romantic music, Zeppo discovers a pretty girl, Mary Helton, the daughter of gangster Joe. Her father is basically a good guy despite his past: he is retiring into high society (another sign of how unworthy of respect it is) and gives generous tips for service. This contrasts with his adversary, the coarse Alky Briggs, who wouldn't hand out a dime and is still in the rackets. It is therefore all right for Zeppo to take an interest in Mary. He tries a gentle ribbing of established romantic routines. "Mighty pretty country around here!" he observes to Mary, indicating the ocean, then asking her if she owns the handkerchief he has just dropped. She rebuffs this attempt to get to know her and walks on. After a few steps her face breaks out in a smile and she drops a flower from her lapel. As Zeppo approaches, she asks if it is his. Zeppo, like Harpo when Penelope dropped her handkerchief as an opening gambit, declares that it does belong to him and takes her arm as she remarks on the lovely trees all around them. This scene is hardly necessary but it is at least disarmingly handled and if there has to be a romantic lead it might as well be Zeppo. The slightly satirical relationship of Zeppo to Mary continues when Zeppo gets around to telling her how much she means to him. "I'll never leave you," he promises but immediately dashes off as some of the crew spot him. And it is Zeppo, the brother best built for a scrap, who completes the fight to save Mary for her kidnappers in the old barn. Groucho, Chico and Harpo merely stand around watching (Groucho doing a 'commentary'), leaving Zeppo to get on with it. Here, in this one film, he seems to find his place and does something essential for the picture.

*   *   *

On breaking free from his brothers, Groucho finds the Captain. At the time the man is chatting with a bevy of young passengers. Groucho cuts a marvellously lecherous figure as he slides down a stair rail to land in their midst and take over. "You girls go to your rooms!" he commands. "I'll be down shortly!" Before long Groucho has simply taken over the boat and ordered the Captain's lunch. He is wearing the Captain's cap at the time. On being asked who it is ordering lunch, he looks at the hatband and replies that he's the Captain. This is a further comment on the problem of identity. If

Abe Cabiddle in *Animal Crackers* can become Roscoe W. Chandler, noted art dealer, just by dressing up for the part, so Groucho can honestly take himself for the Captain by wearing the Captain's mark of office and identifying himself by it (if it were a simple masquerade, he wouldn't bother to check). It emphasises the fallibility of mere appearances as a guide to identity and character.

Soon Groucho is on the run again and he darts into a cabin past Alky Briggs and his wife. They are so busily quarrelling that they scarcely give him a glance as he says "Pardon me while I step into the closet" and darts past them. Only when Alky has stormed out does his wife Lucille investigate the figure who went into the closet. She goes up to it and asks him what he's doing in there. The door opens, Groucho's head pops out, his eyeballs rotate lasciviously, his eyebrows 'superciliate'. "Nothing," he purrs. "Come on in." He later slips out and reclines on the bed as Lucille, shapely but frustrated, calls him Browneyes and asks for his sympathy over Alky's mistreatment of her. Groucho is aroused by her need for excitement and he lays it on the line. "Madam," he declares, "Before I get through with you, you will have a clear case for divorce and so will my wife." Here Groucho's obsession with sex gets tangled up with his eye for a quick buck and he goes off at a tangent. "Now the first thing to do is to arrange for a settlement. You take the children, your husband takes the house, junior burns down the house, you take the insurance and I take you." It all sounds deceptively simple when

MONKEY BUSINESS: A hungry Chico and Groucho prepare to invade the sanctity of the captain's quarters.

put so smoothly, a perfectly logical progression of events. Soon the romantic streak comes out and he dances a tango with her that transports them round the cabin and Groucho across her bed. They separate and Groucho circles on his own, eyes closed, face blissful, whirling past the door where he rejoins his partner. They move across the room together and Groucho pushes out his lips for an ecstatic kiss. This is the closest Groucho ever gets to a moment of real passion as distinct from kicking the idea of it around. But in matters of love and sex, he is always disappointed. Later in the film he emerges from a pile of hay, plaintively inquiring, "Where are all those farmers' daughters I've been reading about?" Here in the cabin he only gets to the point of kissing because he has in fact picked up Lucille's husband at the door and not Lucille herself.

Caught in this very compromising position, Groucho quickly takes the initiative by changing roles with Alky and enacting the injured party. "Sir, this is an outrage, breaking into a man's home!" he barks at Alky, adding, "I'm not in the habit of making threats but there'll be a letter about this in *The Times* tomorrow morning!" Having invoked the power of *The Times*, Groucho exploits the sanctity of motherhood as Alky tells him he won't be reading *The Times* because he'll be laid out pretty by then. "Oh, you're going to lay me out pretty, eh? That's the thanks I get for freeing an innocent girl who, although she's hiding in the closet at the moment, has promised to become the mother of her children." Then, slipping into a gruff Southern accent, he walks stiffly away. "Good day, sir, good day." The richness of all this lies in the fact that not only are *The Times* and motherhood inappropriate to the situation anyway but even if they were they wouldn't affect a bad-tempered, very tough gangster like Alky Briggs.

This entire scene lives up to Perelman's observation about Groucho's character: "His best quality was the ability to turn in his own wheelbase, with a phrase or a movement to set up a whole situation, or to destroy it, or kid it and shift rapidly into another identity or pose." [26]

Groucho now becomes quite sickeningly juvenile. Alky has only to declare that he's wise, meaning that he knows what's been going on behind his back, for Groucho to seize on it. "You're wise, eh? Well, what's the capital of Nebraska? What's the capital of the Chase National Bank? Give up?" This whole business of quizzes which often crops up in the Marx films further exemplifies the low cultural pursuits adhered to by the Marxes. Alky lets Groucho see the gun he has concealed in his pocket. "Cute, isn't it?" says Groucho, peering inside. "Did Santy Claus bring it for Christmas?" Then he twists his body with a proud swagger and tells Alky: "I got a fire engine!" Alky tries a more ferocious expression and bellows, "Do you know who I am?" Groucho covers his head, not from intimidation but so

as to think. "Now don't tell me. Are you animal or vegetable?"
Alky asks if there is anything he has to say before he's drilled.
Groucho's voice goes deep and husky as he replies: "Yes, I'd like
to ask you one question." Then, in a high-pitched semi-gabble, he
says: "Do you think girls think less of a boy if he lets himself be
kissed? I mean, don't you think that although girls go out with boys
like me they always marry the other kind?" It is a fine parody of,
and his voice an apt commentary on, the content and language of the
inane advice columns in juvenile magazines. Alky is so taken back
by Groucho's nerve that he hires him and Zeppo (who dashes in and
shows himself to be Groucho's friend) as bodyguards to help him
strong-arm Joe Helton into handing over control of his gang. About
here, as Helton deals with Zeppo, there is an indelible glimpse of
Groucho in a coy stance, sucking his finger and smirking childishly
— like the whole scene it is hilarious, but semi-nauseating all the
same. It sounded beneath the Marx Brothers but this Groucho one
can readily see as the author of insulting notes to the Captain. There
are later lapses into infantilism — Prime Minister Groucho in *Duck
Soup*, hearing of a political trouble-maker, declares: "I've a good
mind to ring his doorbell and run" — but these are momentary and
not as integral as they are here.

Groucho later comes across Helton reclining in a deck-chair and,
in a scheme comparable to that for an eight-cent nickel in *Animal
Crackers*, he proposes a saving of money and supports his arguments

MONKEY
BUSINESS:
The passport counter
and four songbirds
all masquerading as
Maurice Chevalier
(N.B. It doesn't
happen quite this
way but the still
captures the spirit
of the scene).

with all the slick salesmanship and regard for facts and figures that the hard-headed American businessman requires. "Now there are two fellows trying to attack you, aren't there?" he asks Helton, meaning Zeppo and himself, "And there are two fellows trying to defend you" (meaning Harpo and Chico who have lined up with Helton). He goes on: "Now that's fifty per cent waste. Now why can't you be attacked by your own bodyguard? Your life will be saved and that's a hundred per cent waste. Now what have you got? You've still got me and I'll attack you for nothing." Helton doesn't have a chance to express himself before Groucho declares: "All right, then, it's all settled. I'm to be your new bodyguard. In case I'm going to attack you, I'll have to be there to defend you, too. Now let me know when you want to be attacked and I'll be there ten minutes later to defend you." All the efforts of modern business towards streamlined efficiency and cutting of manpower have to stand aside for Groucho's ideas in economy.

Helton's party (the section of the film following the voyage) presents a lovesick Groucho crawling up and down the verandah wall miaowing into the night as he sees Lucille Briggs approaching. He starts to embrace her on the sofa but she is worried about Alky finding them: "If he finds me out here, he'll wallop me!" "Always thinking of your husband," remonstrates Groucho, "Couldn't I wallop you just as well?" This splendidly erotic suggestion is followed by Groucho's proposal that they should lodge with his fleas in the hills. "I mean, flee to my lodge in the hills," he says correcting himself, but as in the bull and cow idea in *The Cocoanuts*, Groucho's command over words only properly breaks down when some new meaning can be squeezed out in the process. Lucille is again concerned to catalogue her life of woe with Alky: "Four years of neglect! Four years of battling! Four years of heartbreak!..." "That makes twelve years," butts in Groucho, "You must have been married in rompers. Mighty pretty country around there. Do you think you'll ever go back?" Here is a dazzling example of Groucho's technique of working from the *sound* of a word. The word 'rompers' sounds vaguely like a place name (one might think of Yonkers), but it is funnier that the imaginary creations of Edward Lear like his Gromboolian Plain or Chankly Bore because it also has an actual meaning that we've been forced away from. To this writer the word sets off a vision of the green countryside of a Rompers County, from the idea of children romping on grass. There is one dubious aspect to this otherwise brilliant little scene when an elderly couple sneak out for a little illicit pecking and Groucho exploits their nervousness and fear of being exposed. Groucho is doing exactly what they are doing with Alky's wife, they haven't antagonised him in any way, and don't have any pompous ideas about themselves. The slight distaste aroused here only emphasises that Groucho

57

is most enjoyable when tackling those who directly ask for it by their manner towards him, like the ship's captain who disturbs his peace in the hold.

* * *

Chico has very little to do independently of his brothers. His canniness emerges when he is discussing with Joe Helton how tough he and Harpo will be as bodyguards. "Well, you pay a little bit," Chico tells Helton, "We're a little bit tough. You pay very much, we very much tough. You pay too much, we're too much tough How much you pay?" Helton assures Chico he pays plenty. "Well, then we're plenty tough." Chico is not giving anything away for nothing. Later he asks the ex-gang boss about a job for his grandfather. "He puts cheese in-a mousetraps," Chico tells him. "Why, we haven't got any mice here," says Helton, speaking of his new mansion. "That's all right," says Chico, "He brings his own mice with him." However nonsensical an idea it makes as a whole, Chico is never lost for an answer to the details: if there is no house next door, then build one (*Animal Crackers*); if there are no mice, then bring some.

Chico's keen interest in self-preservation is clearly seen when he and Groucho face one of the kidnappers in the old barn. "Go on, you get him," says Chico. "I'll wait for you outside." "Keep out of this loft!" yells the man threateningly from upstairs. "Well, 'tis better to have loft and lost than never to have loft at all," declares Chico, delivering one of his more tolerable puns. Otherwise, he is

MONKEY BUSINESS: Groucho alerts a party guest to an Indian uprising.

burdened with some very feeble examples, at least by today's taste, involving heir, air and hair; and some too exaggerated ones like mistaking vessel for whistle (Chico whistles a bit of 'Sugartime') and mutiny for matinee. These are played straight, though in the very short Chico-Groucho scene, Groucho grows so frustrated by Chico's wilful dumbness that in the end he turns despairingly to the audience and says: "There's my argument — restrict immigration!" This is all the more funny because Groucho is accepting Chico on his own terms as an Italian so as to get a jibe in against him.

Early in the film, the Captain innocently puts himself in the hands of Chico and Harpo who have taken over the barber's shop on board ship. He settles down for a doze after ordering a trim. We get some idea of what he is in for when Harpo ties the cloth around his belly and Chico looks down his throat, declaring that they'll do his tonsils last. They move in first on the Captain's moustache. Throughout the Marx films, and as a key to the Marx world, beards and moustaches are a sign of affectation rather than of virility or manliness and frequently come in for drastic treatment. The Captain's finely cultivated moustache is soon being snipped away and shrinks to Oliver Hardy dimensions (when the plump features of the Captain add to the resemblance). It eventually vanishes altogether as Harpo buries it under shaving lather and whisks it off, swishing lather and whiskers on to the arm rest. Chico looks at it admiringly: "Ah, that's-a beautiful, uh? That's what-a you call a work of art. Hey, you know, I think you give him one snoop too many."

Other victims who are, by their dress and manner, deserving of the attention they receive from Chico and Harpo include a bearded old-timer who has his whiskers tugged in error; a pair of octogenarians who, instead of playing chess in a straightforward manner, do it with pretentious hesitations and tentative gestures with their hands, eventually tiring Chico and Harpo who make moves for them, Harpo taking a piece right off the board; and a haughty opera singer who calls for a doctor and fails to make clear she's not the patient ("Well, we're not the doctor," points out Chico, making a reasonable reply to her indignation after she's been leapt upon by Harpo and otherwise mistreated).

*   *   *

Harpo is at his most savage and inhuman during *Monkey Business*. His costume has become much more flamboyant, simply by the addition of a shirt that screams for colour. His pursuit of women is even more single-minded than before, and culminates in a shot of Harpo on a bicycle relentlessly closing in on a shrieking blonde who is tearing across the lawn away from Joe Helton's party. He is much more infantile, indulging in such pranks as tricking a male passenger into entering the women's lavatory. He hears a steward calling "Tag!" and touches him on the shoulder, then darts away

59

MONKEY BUSINESS: Chico and Harpo sign on as the bodyguards of Joe Helton (Rockcliffe Fellowes).

expecting to be chased in a game of tag. He gets Alky Briggs with
his hands up and starts the patty-cake routine with him. Apart from
the attack on poor Mrs. Rittenhouse, he is much more violent than
he has been before (or will be later). When his attempt to pass
through the Customs as Maurice Chevalier fails, he goes berserk and
flings papers in every direction. As an official tries to drag him away
by grasping him round the waist, the man's hat falls off exposing
a bald head which Harpo frenziedly rubberstamps. We could sympa-
thise with Harpo's destruction of the letters in *The Cocoanuts* or the
telegram in *Duck Soup* — "He gets mad because he can't read,"
explains Chico — but here his destructiveness lacks any such calm
rationalisation and is much more wildly carried out. In his fight
scene with Chico, he is far more ferocious than before, as Chico tells
him to be so as to demonstrate to Joe Helton how tough they'd be as
bodyguards. Instead of kicking Chico, Harpo lets loose a couple of
mighty uppercuts after which Chico looks positively groggy.

Even Harpo's visual puns are less restrained. He loses a pet frog
and overhears a little man (who has already been bowled over during
the chase on deck) saying very hoarsely, "I've got a frog in my
throat". Harpo promptly upends the man, visibly bouncing his head
on the floor, in an attempt to dislodge it. Of course, Roscoe Chandler
was upended in the search for his birthmark but he deserved it.
This little man's only fault is having learned to speak an inexact
language, and he is perhaps one of the few innocent bystanders

caught up in the Marxes' assault on a deserving world. All Harpo's other punning on words is quite harmless (except sometimes with his brothers). More typical are such moments as those in *Horse Feathers* when he brings in a live and indignant seal when Groucho wants to legalise a document or splits a table with an axe when he overhears a gambler say "Cut the cards!" Both are upsetting but neither involves the physical punishment the little guy undergoes here.

There is a very physical quality to another type of situation that starts to appear from *Monkey Business* onwards. This involves bodies being crushed together or at any rate pressing on one another. During a chase on deck Harpo succeeds in hiding from the crew. Once it is safe, a woman in a chair clambers to her feet rather rapidly, revealing Harpo beneath her. When he rushes off, a very squashed figure of an elderly man rises from the depths of the chair. How this human sandwich came into being is not something one questions. Later scenes on a similar line include Harpo's appearance from beneath the Lemonade Seller in his bathtub (*Duck Soup*) and the search of Goliath's apartment by Chico and Harpo (*At the Circus*).

MONKEY BUSINESS: As Joe Helton leaves his cabin, Harpo and Chico prepare for trouble as his bodyguards.

Harpo succeeds in playing the harp at Helton's party by scaring off the accompanist to a soprano solo. His hand materialises on the far side of the harp, plucking the strings; the woman harpist flees and Harpo takes her place, idly scratching the sole of his shoe as if it were an itchy foot, providing a very casual accompaniment and looking annoyed when the soloist seems to prolong her number ('O Sole Mio' — not even in plain English). He is as disinterested in this type of music as Groucho is in introducing the woman. (He performs his own piece at Chico's suggestion — but for his own pleasure, not for Helton's guests.)

At one point here he unscrews his hand and throws it away, letting another hand, his real one, appear out of his sleeve. This is one of the many surrealistic touches in Harpo's work, and in *Monkey Business* there occurs one scene that generates the most bizarre confusion between the animate and the inanimate and falls entirely into the category of surrealism.

MONKEY BUSINESS: A bearded old-timer has his whiskers tugged in error by Harpo and Chico as they mistake him for their boss in disguise.

It is well worth recalling the scene in some detail before commenting on it. It starts with Harpo taking refuge aboard ship in the room where a crowd of small children are being entertained by a Punch and Judy show. He has a paroxysm of laughter as he surveys the show and points his finger at the puppets, fully sharing the children's delight. Then the First Officer arrives outside and decides to look around. He comes to the front of the Punch and Judy show. In the opening are two puppets plus Harpo, his face frozen in the ghastly appearance of a 'gookie'. The other two puppets hit Harpo on the head with sticks; his eyes show mock irritation.

Harpo arouses the First Officer's suspicions and the man goes round the back. Seeing Harpo's posterior jutting out, he takes a large pin from his lapel with a look of impending rich satisfaction and viciously jabs Harpo with it. Harpo turns round anguishedly as the First Officer arrives in front to find his rear now protruding through the stage and hits it with a flat stick. He then grasps Harpo round the neck and is viciously throttling him to the vast amusement of the children who haven't stopped chorusing their delight at what has been going on when the Captain enters and is astonished at this apparent mad fit by one of his officers. "Quiet!" he barks at the kids and starts to ridicule the man who explains he has caught one of the stowaways. But as he is talking Harpo substitutes one of the real puppets. The First Officer seizes it, quite sure of himself, and the puppet squeals a few words of protest as it is being choked. The First Officer stops, knowing now that he has made a mistake, and looks sheepish. "Go to your cabin!" orders the Captain. But then Harpo reappears and the First Officer exclaims, "Look!" Harpo swings his head round as the Captain turns, to show a mask he has fixed to the back of his head (part of a trick in *Duck Soup*). The Captain taps the mask and produces a hollow sound. He looks scornfully at the man when Harpo blows out a toy that touches the back of the Captain's neck. The Captain looks around and pinches the flesh of Harpo's fixed face. He is just saying that the First Officer may be right when Harpo kicks him through the flap in front. The Captain seizes the leg and starts to pull at it energetically with the help of the First Officer. The children roar with excitement and Harpo whistles the men on as they tug at his leg. Then Harpo pops out to help them pull at the leg. Suddenly it comes away and the two men fall on the floor clutching a false leg. Harpo makes a stylish getaway in a miniature engine with a nod to the delighted children.

Besides the sheer brilliance of Harpo's performance with its moments of rigid control (lifelessness) and outbreaks of wild mischief, there are two other points worth noticing. One is that the puppet master, the man who must be there manipulating the puppets, is totally ignored and never seen. Thus the puppets appear to have a life of their own, e.g. the one that protests at being strangled.

(Though this could be Harpo speaking, the puppets were performing when he first came in.) The distinction between the puppets and Harpo is narrowed even further since the puppets go some way towards being human. It took comic acumen to realise that there was no need to explain this point. Secondly, the scene gains a lot from its appreciative on-screen audience. The children cannot distinguish between the performance and the interruptions. This can be taken to reveal the sadistic delights of children or as a reminder of the viciousness of Punch and Judy shows. We don't question the children's response because we can see how virtually indistinguishable the people and the puppets have become — through Harpo's impersonation and the clownish behaviour of all three men. And the acceptance of these actions by the children nudges us into being more ready to laugh at them ourselves.

Nowhere in this film are there the little sympathetic flashes that make Harpo 'human', like in *Duck Soup*, when Harpo plays Groucho's mirror image, his face drops momentarily into a gleeful chuckle as his true self slips through, allowing us to identify with his very human delight in the game. Here in *Monkey Business*, Joe Helton presents to his guests at the party "The most beautiful thing in the world" and Harpo steps forward to take a bow in place of his daughter. It registers as the grossest impertinence of Harpo's career.

* * *

MONKEY BUSINESS: Harpo, disguised as a bustle, attaches himself to a woman guest at Joe Helton's party.

"I was doing this kind of comedy long before I met S. J. Perelman," said Groucho recently, and added: "Everybody has some kind of a curious notion that we were — or I was — deeply influenced by Perelman. That's not true at all. We're good friends but he wrote very little for us. As a matter of fact he wasn't great for us. We had writers — stage writers — that were much better for us than Sid. Now nobody could write a funnier piece than Sid but he wasn't really a constructionist for the stage . . . The best writers we had were Kaufman and Ryskind."

Any direct influence by Perelman cannot be dated earlier than this film and it could only extend over one further film, *Horse Feathers*. Neither of these did he solely script and on both he worked with Will B. Johnstone, who had a similar writing background to Perelman. Both these pictures are distinctive in lacking Margaret Dumont, but *Monkey Business* goes further, to stand quite apart from the other Marx work in ways that might well be attributable to Perelman. It has the sharp tang of a malicious and mocking eye and is less comfortable and less good-natured than the rest. It has qualities in common with Perelman's literary output. Groucho's puerile, somewhat nauseating but highly comic manner (which doesn't even recur in *Horse Feathers*) seems to bear the stamp of Perelman, as could the more savage, more demoniacal Harpo of this film. Summing it up, the team becomes much less sympathetic, indeed rather ruthlessly *un*sympathetic — which may or may not be an improvement but which is a distinctive feature.

Horse Feathers is more in the spirit of the first two Marx films by Kaufman and Ryskind: more of a vehicle, more solidly and conventionally constructed, as though Kalmar and Ruby, with their vaudeville background, approached the script with audience satisfaction first in their minds while Johnstone and Perelman, principally journalists, tended to write more for themselves, more for minority tastes. For *Monkey Business* isn't played to an audience like the other films. It has a 'take it or leave it' air but on its own terms it has a lot to be said for it.

6. Horse Feathers (1932)

*M*onkey Business represented a break with the stagebound, hermetic world of a grossly caricatured high society both in its wider range of settings and in its characters. The gangsters, one seeking respectability, and the wife yearning for kicks, had some closer connection with the times, but Groucho looked on occasion somewhat reduced by these determined figures even if his brothers had no difficulties. In *Horse Feathers* the Marxes all reach their full stature and the area of attack is much wider: education, sport, love and the Depression all come under accurate and devastating fire. It is the first of the Marx films to really satirise the period. But in retrospect *Horse Feathers* falls short of its promise. It doesn't have

Left, MONKEY BUSINESS: the burlesque tango. Groucho partners Thelma Todd as Lucille Briggs. Right, HORSE FEATHERS: the intrepid Miss Todd again, this time as Connie Bailey. Harpo is wearing Groucho's gum shoes and an expression that spells danger for Connie.

HORSE FEATHERS: Groucho, backed up by the bearded
professors, sings in the opening scene when he is installed as
the new president of Huxley College.

the drive and impact of *Duck Soup* which reflects a difference in
direction and construction. Norman McLeod (who seems to have
been more suited to *Monkey Business*) has a looser script and doesn't
impose himself as firmly as Leo McCarey does in driving *Duck Soup*
fast and furious to a rousing finale.

*   *   *

The education aspect is most central to *Horse Feathers* and brings
us to the core of the Marx philosophy, for it is learning of various
kinds that makes certain people consider themselves superior to
others. The Marxes believe in a natural wisdom and practical skills,
not the posturings of the well-bred (who buy a good education) or the
obscure knowledge of the dull pedant. Harpo cannot even write his
name but he has no trouble getting along in the world. Groucho has
become the new President of Huxley College (though they've been
one a year since 1888) and he quickly shows what he thinks of
higher education and the people that teach it. The film starts with a
kind of inauguration ceremony, but less elaborate than that of *Duck
Soup*. The professors seated on the platform are all bearded (except
for the retiring President, but his pronounced growth of side-whiskers
is just as bad and besides he's only had a year there). They specifically forbid smoking. Groucho, as Professor Quincey Adams Wag-

67

staff, is first seen *shaving* in the corner of the stage, i.e. emphasising the difference between himself and them. His moustache may represent his assuming the society appearance but it has the impermanence of greasepaint and a distinctly unrefined shape. He carries on smoking his cigar throughout the scene.

His address to the assembled students soon degenerates into another spot of auctioneering. "Any questions?" he asks. "Any answers? Let's have some action around here. Who'll say 76? Who'll say 17.76? That's the spirit! 1776!" (i.e. 'The Spirit of '76', the date of the Declaration of Independence being 1776). He starts a conversation with Zeppo, playing his student son (ingenious and absurd: Groucho, of course, looks too young to have a son of Zeppo's age). The retiring President of the college interrupts to tell Groucho, "I am sure the students would appreciate a brief outline of your plans for the future." "What?" barks Groucho. The man repeats himself word for word. "You just said that! That's the trouble around here: talk, talk, talk!" exclaims Groucho, having by this almost infallible method shown professors to be long-winded and repetitive. In a later scene, a pair of professors show themselves to be simply yes-men, prepared to agree with whatever Groucho says in order to safeguard their academic careers, regardless of what education needs.

During the opening scene, Groucho expounds his philosophy in song. It is a nihilistic one well suggested by the title, 'I'm Against It'. Whatever the college professors have to say, he's opposed to it. During the number, Groucho dances around tugging the line of scraggy beards on the seated academics while the students make up a chorus enthusiastically echoing Groucho's words. The Professors themselves join in the number, shifting around the stage like sheep, too weak-willed to resist the mood of the moment.

Later in the film, Chico and Harpo are signed up as students purely so that they can play football for the college, another hint of how farcical the education system is. When it comes to signing a contract, all Harpo can do is put a cross, yet he is enrolled for advanced instruction. Later on, he does his best to bring education down to his

HORSE
FEATHERS:
This impish Harpo
has taken the law
into his own hands.

HORSE
FEATHERS:
Harpo orders a
drink in the
speakeasy. With
Groucho, Chico,
then Vince Barnett.

own level by vigorously shovelling books on the fire in Groucho's study. It is a little unfortunate that Harpo's actions foreshadow Nazi methods of mass-burning books to suppress culture.

The fullest attack on education is made by all three brothers during the biology lecture. The professor in charge, though barely recognisable beneath a feature-obliterating set of whiskers, is played by Robert Greig, the head butler in *Animal Crackers* and the embodiment of solemn dignity in many of the Preston Sturges comedies. In *Horse Feathers*, his deep, booming voice and his manner are ideal to suggest the solemn lecturer. Groucho enters to ask, "Have they started sawing the woman in half yet?". He expects the classroom to be as entertaining as a magician's act, and equally as deceitful. He brings in Chico and Harpo as new students who give the professor a gift as though this were an infant's school. Soon they are fighting with each other, Harpo threatening to punch Chico and switching to a kick. Groucho looks at a slide through the microscope and remarks, "Well, I'd say it came in second but it was very close", which lets a whiff of the racetrack pervade the sacred atmosphere of higher learning. The professor resumes his lecture but his words are technical and without ordinary meaning so that Groucho wonders if he isn't making it all up, a suspicion often voiced by those who like to defend their ignorance. The professor assures Groucho that his students will bear him out. Sure enough, Harpo and Chico bear him out into the corridor, and Groucho, in academic robes incongruously topped by a cloth cap (the man in the street) rather than a mortar board, takes over the lecture, improvising as he points around on a chart of the human body: "Now the blood carriers are a hill-dwelling tribe that live in the Alps. They feed on rice and old shoes. Then behind the Alps is more Alps and the Lord alps those who alp themselves [a line originally used in *I'll Say She Is*]. The blood rushes from the head to the feet, gets a look at those feet, and then rushes back up to the head again." Harpo slips out and substitutes first a picture of a horse, then a pin-up in place of Groucho's chart. He shyly confesses to being the culprit, crying like a repentant child as Groucho tells him: "My boy, as you grow older, you'll find you can't burn the candle at both ends." At this, Harpo's face lights up with glee and he produces a candle lit at both ends. He has caught the professor out and, like the child who contradicts his teacher on one small point, can consider to have dismissed the whole lesson. He has disproved the saying on its most literal level, showing how often words are used thoughtlessly to convey more meaning than they are basically equipped to do. As Groucho resumes the lesson, he has lost whatever respect Harpo had and it degenerates into a battle with pea-shooters. Groucho tries to ignore the rain of peas, then, working' round to a defensive position, he returns the fire and succumbs to the primitive pleasures of pea-shooting. The improvement of the mind has been entirely abandoned.

A speakeasy figures in part of the film. Chico works as its general help and, in a satiric comment on the times, pours the same liquid into two bottles labelled Scotch and Rye, implying that their taste was identical in the days of bootleg liquor. He then has to watch the door and see that newcomers know the password 'swordfish'. Groucho knocks. Chico eyes him through the opening and asks, "Who are you?" To which Groucho replies: "I'm fine thanks, who are you?" It is only to be expected that when Groucho does give a straight answer for once it should be to a different question. Groucho admits he doesn't know the password but Chico gives him a sporting chance: three guesses. For a clue, he's told that it's the name of a fish. Groucho guesses "sturgeon" which Chico takes to be "surgeon". "Haddock" is merely a "headache" to Chico who gives him a bit of further advice: "You can't come in unless you say 'swordfish'." Groucho gets it right on the next guess and enters, shutting the door on Chico, who knocks, gives the password, but is refused admittance by Groucho who has changed the word. "Well, what's the new one?" asks Chico. "Gee, I forgot it," replies Groucho, "I'd better come out there with you." Both end up locked out, a typically fruitless encounter. It is even retrogressive because Chico was originally inside. The last line is rather weak — it suggests that as Groucho doesn't know the password he isn't entitled to be inside and so comes out — but it doesn't immediately register in this way and it is unlike Groucho to concede such a point.

When they eventually get inside, Chico learns that Groucho is looking for a couple of footballers who hang around there. "We always hang around here," says Chico of himself and Harpo. "Well, that's all I want to know," says Groucho and promptly signs them up as his football players. It is the same kind of illogical thinking that Groucho makes in signing up "the greatest tenor in the world" in *A Night at the Opera* for Chico is no more the manager of the singer Groucho means than he is a football player here. Groucho also comes off worst as far as paying for the drinks is concerned. Chico makes a show of democratically tossing for it but conceals the result from Groucho, telling him he's lost. "Can you cash a check for fifteen dollars and twenty-two cents?" asks Groucho of the bartender who opens his cash register. Groucho adjusts his glasses, very patiently waiting, clearly master of the situation. He takes the money from the bartender and declares as he makes off that as soon as a check for that amount comes along the man will be sure to get it.

* * *

Harpo has no trouble with speakeasy doors. He carries a fish with a sword in its throat to gain admission. Inside he orders a scotch by dancing a highland jig, empties the one-arm bandit and the telephone of loose coins, letting the money gush out all over him like a refreshing spray from a water fountain, and swindles the bar out of a bottle of liquor.

In this film he is not as unsympathetic as he was in *Monkey Business* but there is nothing about him that is lovable or likable. There is no sympathetic response to his crying over missing a football match; instead he seems a spoilt and unruly child who could benefit from a little deprivation after having everything his own way. His costume has become far scruffier making him more uncouth than ever. His trousers are split so that the ends flap as he moves, his coat is slashed, his braces dangle loosely, his wig looks like an old mop.

By occupation, he is a dog-catcher: the first time he has had a job. To this lowly work he brings a fiendish cunning. He lures one wire-terrier into his cart by simply letting it chase him there. It is

HORSE FEATHERS: Thelma Todd, Chico, and Groucho. The college president has lost the college widow to the iceman. Harpo has his turn later (see an earlier still).

clear when he goes after an alsatian sitting patiently on the other side of the street that he doesn't restrict himself to strays but rounds up every dog in sight. He has a consistent dislike for dogs and he probably works more for the pleasure than for the money. He carries a set of different sized fake lamp posts to interest dogs and lies in wait for them like a big-game hunter. Unfortunately the version of *Horse Feathers* released to television only takes up this scene at the very end when a tramp asks Harpo for help to get a cup of coffee. Harpo demonstrates his complete control over reality (as Chico remarked, "He's got everything") by producing one, hot and steaming, from his raincoat pocket. This is *not* generosity on Harpo's part. Like the burning candle, he only does it to confound the man who would almost certainly have used a hand-out to buy liquor.

HORSE FEATHERS: Groucho takes an interest in the biology lesson. Beneath the whiskers, Robert Greig plays the professor in charge.

It is a pity this establishing scene with Harpo has been lost on many prints because it shows us how obsessive Harpo's pursuit of dogs is so that we understand his immediate reaction to the distant bark of a dog. Harpo's dislike of dogs is balanced by his affection for horses. Zeppo sings a love song ('Everyone Says "I Love You"')

72

that dissolves into Harpo whistling it at the kerb side, looking up at his horse who pulls his dog-cart. He extends a bunch of flowers towards his beloved who starts munching them. He then offers a bag of oats which the horse declines until they are sprinkled with salt. Harpo and the animal tuck into the oats and look a well-matched pair — the horse being part-human in insisting on the salt, but Harpo going furthest in eating the meal.

Unfortunately the picnic is holding up a long line of traffic. A cop comes over and Harpo invites him to join them. The man angrily starts to write out a summons and Harpo's imitative abilities are finely displayed as he makes a game out of the policeman's every action. He dabs his tongue with a pencil and furiously scribbles a note to hand the cop. They exchange bits of paper. The cop tears his up and Harpo does likewise. The policeman displays his badge: Harpo outsmarts him by opening his coat (as with similar challenges in *The Cocoanuts* and *At the Circus*). Inside are hundreds of police badges. The cop makes a threatening motion with his nightstick. Harpo grasps the free end and shakes hands with it, then, when the cop pulls it back into an upright position, grabs it at a point just above where the cop's hand is, letting them next proceed hand over fist up the stick as Harpo and Penelope did with her cane in *The Cocoanuts*.

*   *   *

Love enters the picture with Zeppo's romancing of the college widow, Connie Bailey. The film hardly clears up the obscurity to foreign audiences of what a college widow is, but leaves the impression that she is a woman of rather loose morals. Thelma Todd, who played Lucille Briggs in *Monkey Business*, undertakes Connie and comes in for the amorous attentions of all four Marx Brothers and not just Groucho. Her valiant bearing under the range of indignities that afflict her in these two films deserves a special tribute here as her death in 1935 cut short a promising career.

Connie, the character, deserves all she gets as she is working in cahoots with Jennings, head of Huxley's rival, Darwin College. Zeppo shows his interest in her openly but Harpo materialises hanging on a coat peg as Jennings takes away his overcoat and leaves. Harpo slips down to the floor and sneaks across to kiss Connie soundly on the neck while she still thinks Jennings is there, then rushes back as Zeppo enters. Again, Harpo is shown, in stealing the kiss, to be bashful with particular women (cf. Penelope in *The Cocoanuts*) and only lusts openly after beautiful strangers. (Later Harpo serenades Connie on the harp, becoming a most respectful suitor and breaking a pattern whereby, even at the party in *Monkey Business*, he was really playing for himself.)

Zeppo goes to pour drinks and Groucho arrives to express his concern over Zeppo's interest in her: "Whatever you say is a lie. He's

HORSE FEATHERS: Groucho tries to gain entrance to a
speakeasy, negotiating his way past Chico's lookout.

only a shell of his former self which nobody can deny. Whoopee!" He
sits down on *her* lap and makes the practical observation: "I could
sit here all day if you didn't stand up." His lines about Zeppo are
booby-trapped with the phrase "which nobody can deny" that doesn't
really mean anything but seems somehow very forceful; perhaps
we don't notice it, perhaps we know all along, or perhaps we realise
on further thought that this is something we've sung many times
over as "For he's a jolly good fellow *which nobody can deny*" without really hearing the words. Groucho's "Whoopee" distracts one
from dwelling on the matter, but this is a good example of how language can gain an automatic response that bypasses the mind.

A knock on the door sends Groucho into hiding and Harpo enters,
making the first of several appearances carrying a block of ice
(as though anticipating the title of Eugene O'Neill's play *The Iceman
Cometh*). Harpo leaves. Groucho appears, and Zeppo enters with the
drinks. He finds Groucho on Connie's lap but becomes the victim of
his technique of reversing roles as Groucho enacts the outraged
father who has caught his son. "Oh, the shame of it!" he cries,
slipping into a theatrical pose with his back towards Zeppo. Zeppo
and Groucho leave, Groucho returns, then Chico enters carrying a
block of ice (as though it were an admission ticket to the proceedings). He throws it out of the window and, revealing for once an

amorous streak, leaps on Connie, kissing her neck, leaving Groucho glumly edged out. Harpo comes and goes with ice. Jennings returns. "This must be the main highway," remarks Groucho. Chico poses as Connie's music teacher, sings a variation of 'Everyone Says "I Love You" ' with some nonsensical lyrics, and gets on famously with her, pinching her cheek. He then begins his regular piano piece and Groucho and Jennings sit despondently listening. Groucho advances to camera and slips in one of his sharpest cracks at Chico by advising us, "I've got to stay here but there's no reason why you folks shouldn't go out into the lobby until this thing blows over." Groucho's sharing his thoughts with us is one of the main ways (together with the humiliation he suffers in the hands of his brothers at times) that make him seem human. Jennings eventually turns Chico and Groucho out as he leaves himself. This is the only scene in which all four Marx brothers appear, apart from the climactic football game (and in both Zeppo disappears from view for long spells). In its accelerated bedroom farce, it is very similar (though less rapid) to the scene in *The Cocoanuts* in the bedrooms of Penelope and Mrs. Potter.

HORSE FEATHERS: Harpo, dog catcher extraordinary, with a meal and a bunch of flowers for his beloved horse.

HORSE FEATHERS:
Jennings (David Landau)
looks puzzled in Connie's
apartment. The Marxes
look unusually thought-
ful. Connie looks
worried.

The television copy ends it here but actually the sequence goes on, first with Harpo and Connie, and the cut version deprives Harpo of another of his best scenes. "What do you want?" asks Connie sharply as Harpo reappears. Harpo points at her. Connie decides, like Penelope, to play up to him. "Are you a good boy?" she asks, and Harpo shakes his head. "You're bashful," she observes, presumably because he hasn't spoken. In answer, Harpo nods, looks bashful, and stands on his head in Connie's lap. She cries for him to get off her and he does, sitting alongside her on the sofa with one foot tucked under him. She tells him to take his foot off the sofa. Harpo shakes his head defiantly and makes his 'gookie' expression, so she tries to pull it off. Harpo pulls her leg in return. She slaps him, a knock is heard, and he pulls her on to his lap. It is Groucho looking for his hat and rubbers. Connie points in one direction while the hidden Harpo points in another. Connie seems to be slapping herself as Harpo's hands become playful. "Come now, where's my hat?" asks Groucho and Connie seems to point in three directions at once. Groucho finds his rubbers on Harpo's feet, sticking out from under-

76

neath Connie, and mistakes them for hers. Eyeing the expanse of
muscular leg (Harpo's trousers are rolled up), he comments, "We
could use you in the football team." Groucho takes off the rubbers
and tries to put them on his own feet; but Harpo's feet are so posi-
tioned that he puts them back where they came from, on Harpo.
Chico and Jennings come back. Connie stands up, revealing Harpo,
clutching a block of ice beneath her. Groucho rushes to the window
while Chico and Harpo dart out of the door. Arriving below the
window, Chico encourages Groucho to jump. Harpo brings out a
dog catcher's net to arrest his fall. Groucho jumps. Harpo hears a
dog barking and gives chase, letting Groucho thud to the ground.

Again in this scene a very physical quality is evident: in Harpo
standing on Connie's lap or sitting beneath her, in Groucho thudding
to the ground. The latter in particular produces a rather sickening
sensation, as does Groucho's descent in the lift in *A Night in
Casablanca* after Harpo severs the cable somewhere about the twentieth floor. Harpo and Chico's own arrival in the midst of a ladies'

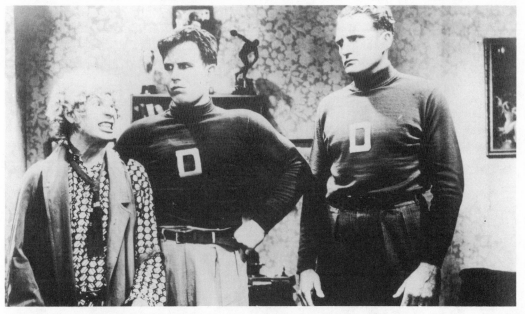

HORSE FEATHERS: Harpo attempts to look ferocious to
Mullen and MacHardie (Nat Pendleton, left, James Pierce, right).

bridge party via a collapsing ceiling later on in the film is somewhat
similar. Connie comes in for a full share when Groucho, Harpo and
Chico marry her simultaneously (pushing the unseen, genuine bridegroom — Zeppo? — out of the way), leaping on top of her to
close the film. This is not really in character (though *A Night in*

Casablanca brings off a similar ending more successfully). Zeppo probably deserves to get Connie (suitably reformed, of course); without him, it would be more likely that Groucho and Chico would start negotiating for her, letting the more impetuous Harpo take some positive action (like his tearing Gottlieb's coat to end *A Night at the Opera*).

A second element that appears in the scene is the familiar one of confusion of identity. Groucho fails to distinguish between Harpo and Connie when they are one on top of the other, and can't tell his own feet from those of Harpo. However impossible this might be in reality, it is played out so plausibly on screen that it has an upsetting, surrealistic effect.

* * *

Jennings wants to know Huxley's football signals to ensure that Darwin are victorious and he can collect on a bet. (Groucho may be an incompetent college head but Jennings, despite a more respectable demeanour, is no better than a crook.) Connie is persuaded to try and pry the signals out of Groucho and makes him take her out on the river. He strums his guitar, warbling the film's love song (so that all four of the Marxes have performed versions of it), then throws the guitar overboard like the cigarette lighter he throws away after use in *Monkey Business*. These actions, and Harpo's silencing

HORSE FEATHERS: Harpo pretends to be coyly embarrassed and he and Chico are stripped of their clothes.

an alarm clock by hitting it with a mallet in *A Night at the Opera*, are in amusingly sharp contrast with the forced economies of the Depression and presage the present 'waste economy' in a mere exaggeration of the new-car-every-year philosophy (a new alarm clock every morning, etc.). They also emphasise the Marx disregard for bourgeois values. The Marxes don't live to conserve wealth and property.

"This is the first time I've been out in a canoe since I saw the

HORSE FEATHERS: Chico and Harpo saw their way out of a tight spot.

American Tragedy," Groucho tells Connie in the film's direct allusion to the school of sombre writing. He then adds a rare line of dubious humour: "I was going to get a flat bottom but the girl at the boat house didn't have one." (The best example is Margaret Dumont innocently asking as they board ship in *A Night at the Opera*, "Have you got everything?" and Groucho replying, "Well, I haven't had any complaints yet"). Connie's remark that Groucho is full of whimsy has one contemplating the sound of the word as Groucho replies as though whimsy were bad breath or a ruddy complexion. Connie is reduced to a little girl act: "Is great big stwong man going to show little icky baby all about the bad football signals?" Groucho answers in an even more excruciatingly babyish voice: "If icky girl keep on talking that way, big stwong man going to kick all her teeth wight down her thwoat." A kicking gesture emphasises the point. Here, beyond the jarring voice, the adult viciousness of the threat contrasts with the infantile voice in which it is expressed (one suspects the hand of Perelman). Connie falls overboard trying to take the football signals away and cries for help: "Professor Wagstaff!" Groucho chooses this moment to quibble about how she should address him, suggesting Quincey and later Quince. Gallantry is not one of Groucho's strong points and he remains seated. The only time in his screen career that he makes a point of it is during this film's climax when he is talking with her at the edge of the field. "Excuse me," he says as a Darwin football player rushes down the pitch with the ball. He runs out, cutting a bizarre figure (properly dressed for the game but for his cigar, frockcoat and an outsize helmet), tackles the man successfully, rubs his hands together, and walks back to the stands. "That'll teach him not to pass a lady without tipping his hat," declares Groucho.

Groucho's methods become as dirty as those of Jennings when he sends Chico and Harpo to kidnap the star football players of the other team. Chico, according to plan, asks the two men if they have a brother. They haven't. A sister then? One of them admits to having a sister. "You got to come with us," exclaims Chico, "Your sister, she's a very sick man." Here, as in the concession Chico makes Harpo in *The Cocoanuts* (he'd kill him for money; no, Harpo's a friend; he'll kill him for nothing), we see the extreme slowness of Chico's mind adjusting to any change in his set ideas.

The plan will not work, so Chico, looking out for himself as usual, pushes Harpo forward to deal with the two tough guys, giving his prizefighter last-minute instructions (cf. Harpo's fight with Mrs. Rittenhouse). Harpo's efforts to become ferocious have him heaving away again, about to foam at the mouth, but at the last minute his playful streak breaks through and he merely gives the pair a cheeky tap. They let loose with a mighty uppercut and Harpo lands on the floor. We really expect him to manage some stratagem to give him at least temporary command (like the pitchfork in the old barn in *Monkey Business*) but he and Chico merely turn tail and run. Chico is rather cruelly humiliated by being upended and tipped out of his clothes, but at least Harpo finds it uproariously amusing and in his turn detaches his outer clothing in one lot and enjoys himself pretending to be coyly embarrassed in his underwear. It is, however, the first time Harpo and Chico have ever suffered any such setback.

* * *

The vital football match provides the climax to *Horse Feathers*.

Chico and Harpo escape, Harpo driving a garbage cart like a chario-
teer entering the arena. Groucho gives instructions to the other
side and Zeppo points out his mistake (as he lets Groucho know he's
machine-gunning his own men in *Duck Soup*). Groucho's comeback
is reasonable enough but the film's director carelessly lets the Darwin
players laugh at his expense, making him look small. Soon after he
is in the stands, stopping long enough to speak to the radio fans in
another example of his climactic commentaries.

Harpo gets his revenge on the two Darwin players. One he brings
down in a classic flying tackle, even though the man hasn't got the
ball at the time. Then there is one diabolical image of Harpo exact-
ing retribution (Perelman, no doubt) which comes as Harpo, playing
and eating a hot dog, is involved in a massive pile-up on the field.
He sits up to find one of the two star players lying dazed and his roll
without its hot dog. He carefully smears mustard on from a pot he
carries, wraps the roll around the man's index finger and takes a
fiendish bite. He did bite Hennessy's finger when it was pointed at
him in *The Cocoanuts* but here the mustard adds a special relish:
this act of cannibalism is a connoisseur's delight — also another of
the 'physical' images that makes one wince in empathy with his
victim.

HORSE FEATHERS: Groucho delivers a commentary during
the climactic football match.

It is Harpo's inventiveness that wins the game for Huxley. He spreads banana skins behind him, attaches elastic to the ball, and otherwise makes a great effort until something more vital — a loose dog — takes his attention. Harpo leaps into his 'chariot' with his brothers and races up the field. At the far end he finds time to unload some footballs behind the goal, raising the Huxley score with each of them.

The game is won but the methods are so blatantly irregular that this tends to diminish our pleasure in the final victory. In no other Marx film is the climax so completely contrived. However impossible (and in part possible, perhaps), the climaxes of such films as *A Night at the Opera* and *A Day at the Races* — to take comparably spectacular endings — do have a superficial plausibility. They *look* possible whereas that of *Horse Feathers* is just too artificially worked out (though not in the same way as those in the much later films where there is trick work that mars our pleasure much more seriously).

7. Duck Soup (1933)

*D*uck Soup stands apart from the other Marx Brothers films. It represents the only occasion that the team were guided by a director with a real genius for comedy: Leo McCarey, who made *The Kid from Spain, Ruggles of Red Gap* and *The Awful Truth,* among others. Also, *Duck Soup* is the only Marx film to have a completely mythical background: a postage-stamp republic called Freedonia. It creates an ideal world in which the four Marxes —

DUCK SOUP: "We fool-a you good, eh, boss?" asks Chico, turning Harpo the right way round and removing his own mask as they report to Ambassador Trentino about their spying.

especially Groucho as President — can operate. While the setting is different, there is no real attempt to create an entirely different society. The Marxes appear in traditional costume. Margaret Dumont, as the wealthiest widow in the land, is unchanged in manner (though hers is a smoother performance in a role she hadn't played on stage). Her name, Gloria Teasdale, is hardly 'Freedonian' and other names, like Trentino and Vera Marcal, are just roughly European. The Lemonade Seller could have come from the Coney Island boardwalk, as could Chico and Harpo's peanut stall. There is some suggestion of backwardness — a motorbike provides the Presidential transport — but tanks and shells feature in the war scenes. While it might seem too absurd if Groucho were President of the U.S.A., there is no difficulty in accepting him as the leader of a mythical country. Just as he was the latest in a long line of college heads at Huxley, so here as Rufus T. Firefly he seems to get his chance partly because everyone else has failed, and partly because it is the condition of Mrs. Teasdale's pouring another twenty million dollars into the Freedonian treasury. She has a belief in him and the people aren't invited to give their opinion. So, instead of being in a peripheral position to the plot (the theft of jewels, the shenanigans with a painting, the internecine quarrel of gangsters, intrigue over football), Groucho moves right to the centre of the stage. Only Chico and Harpo stand up against his power and prove once again to be more than a match for him. They are working openly for Freedonia (Harpo as presidential chauffeur, Chico as Minister of War) and secretly against it (as spies employed by Ambassador Trentino from neighbouring Sylvania). Other plotters against Freedonia receive little space and it is the Marxes themselves who create almost all of the situations in the film. Most spectacularly, it is Groucho who engineers the climactic warfare single-handedly despite both countries' efforts to prevent conflict. Here, in a short, tightly made film, the Marxes are at their most overwhelming.

Groucho's inauguration ceremony is modelled on the opening of *Animal Crackers* and the party scene of *The Cocoanuts*. Trentino quickly shows himself to be a menace to Freedonia, allowing us to

DUCK SOUP: Harpo is distracted by Trentino's blonde secretary.

side with Groucho when he takes a firm dislike to the man. Zeppo is once more the first to arrive and again plays Groucho's assistant (his secretary). He delivers a couple of lines, misplacing the emphasis and sounding most awkward. Then the film moves into Kalmar-Ruby's musical number which, like their 'Hooray for Captain Spaulding', involves the idea of repetition. Here the guests keep singing the national anthem and bowing while Groucho fails to materialise. He eventually slides down an unlikely fire-pole from his upstairs bedroom into the spacious hall and lines up with his own guard of honour.

Groucho is at great pains to dispel any idea that he will be a mature and responsible leader. His ideas for running the country, expressed in song, are tyrannical, chaos-inducing and self-interested. They express the Marx (and anarchist) view that authority means abuse and corruption. When power is placed in Groucho's hands, he expresses this view to an extreme, here in words, later in the war he causes. This time he is fighting authority from the inside, by *his own* misuse of it. He attacks the idea whereas normally he attacks the people that have the power instead of being one of them himself.

He is childish again, reacting peevishly when the Ambassador of Sylvania, Trentino, dismisses his card trick instead of playing along with him. (A little indulgence or liking for cards on the Ambassador's part might have saved him from Groucho's dislike and, as they say, changed the course of history.) Groucho also keeps the whole cabinet waiting while he bounces a ball and tries to scoop up a handful of jacks before catching it.

Diplomacy is an art quite beyond his reach. He is rude even to his most loyal follower, Mrs. Teasdale (cf. his scorn over Mrs. Rittenhouse's efforts to boost his reputation in *Animal Crackers*). "The future of Freedonia rests on you," she declares grandly. "Promise me you will follow in the footsteps of my husband." "How do you like that?" Groucho asks us, looking into camera, "I haven't been on the job five minutes and already she's making advances to me." But pretty soon *he's* making advances to her while making the same check as he did with Mrs. Rittenhouse on her financial status,

DUCK SOUP:
The Ambassador watches his spies with curiosity as Harpo tries to light a cigar with the telephone and Chico tells him, "That's-a no good."

then passing it off as a declaration of love.

Later on he asks her if he might have a lock of hair, then explodes her pleasure by adding: "I'm letting you off lightly — I was going to ask for the whole wig." A moment later he is shown sitting on *her* lap, reversing roles as he did with Connie Bailey, or when in the life he foresaw with Mrs. Potter, it was she who went out to do the day's work while he waited at the garden gate. As in *The Cocoanuts*, he approaches the point of battling with Margaret Dumont. He is about to storm off in a huff when Mrs. Teasdale tries to detain him by pulling at his frock coat. He whirls around, fists ready, then recovers himself and tries to change the atmosphere by bowing deeply. (When a bell rings at his bedside, he sits up, in nightshirt and nightcap, fists ready. This echo of a pugilistic career is ludicrous — and therefore funny — because it is so unbelievable in this puny and cowardly figure; it takes us by surprise because it is not a pretence but a subconscious reaction, at which level it just does not make sense.)

Groucho loses his temper with Trentino but the Ambassador is anxious to patch up their differences without losing face (he wants to take over the country by underhand methods rather than start a war). Groucho agreeably laughs away their silly tiff until, under his careful prompting, Trentino recalls the word which offended Groucho so that the row can explode all over again. Trentino has his face slapped by Groucho's gloves (looking curiously like banana skins in his breast pocket) and departs bellowing, "This means WAR!" (a line that Groucho revives in similar circumstances during *A Night at the Opera*).

Mrs. Teasdale persuades Trentino to attempt another reconciliation and brings Groucho the good news: "I've talked to Ambassador Trentino and he says Sylvania doesn't want war either." Just as he quibbled over how Connie should address him as she was drowning, so on the brink of war Groucho questions Mrs. Teasdales's way of pronouncing 'either' before he magnanimously offers to forget it. As he contemplates her news, we see how Groucho can work quite independently of the other person (he does so earlier by dictating his own invitation to Mrs. Teasdale's party, then accepting it). He simply imagines the other person's actions as he would like to, and then reacts to them himself. So his mood changes from sweetness to rage in a long monologue and as Trentino walks in at the end, arm outstretched, Groucho slaps his face again. (Groucho himself uses this technique brilliantly at the start of his book *Many Happy Returns*, first of all pampering the prospective buyer — 'Dear Reader' — but then as he contemplates him further, as a man having a free browse, ends up by addressing him as 'Swine'.)

* * *

Trentino fares no better with his own staff. When Harpo and Chico come to make their report, they exploit every opportunity to turn the occasion into a game. Trentino invites them to sit. They both choose his chair, he sits down on them, and Chico starts singing 'Rockabye Baby'. He has only to put his cigar down for a moment to have Harpo knock it sharply into a corner of the room, rush around and be declared out by Chico, acting the umpire in their impromptu game of baseball. He has merely to inquire about Firefly's record for Harpo to produce a gramophone record and hand it to him. He has no sooner flung it away in exasperation than Harpo has shot it down with a rifle, Chico rung a bell on his desk, handed Harpo a cigar as a prize, then shut Trentino's cigar box on its owner's fingers. (It recalls Harpo's sharpshooting which won him a cigar in *The Cocoanuts;* it is comparable, too, to the fairground atmosphere Harpo and Chico bring to the old barn in *Monkey Business,* rotating a wheel and stunning the villains.)

Chico eventually delivers his report which shows him taking pride in his own stupidity and feeble sense of humour, much to Trentino's disappointment. "Well, you remember you gave us a picture of this man and said follow him. Well, we get on the job right away and in the one hour — even less than one hour . . ." "Yes?" says Trentino excitedly, as Chico continues: ". . . we lose-a the picture. That's pretty good work, huh?" Trentino insists on a detailed report. "All right, I tell you," replies Chico. "Monday we watch-a Firefly's house but he no come out — he wasn't home. Tuesday we

DUCK SOUP: Harpo versus the Lemonade Seller (Edgar Kennedy).

went to a ballgame but he fool us — he no show up. Wednesday he go to the ballgame and we fool him — we no show up. Thursday was a double-header — nobody show up. Friday it rained all day — there was no ballgame so we stayed home and we listened to it over the radio." "Then you didn't shadow Firefly!" exclaims Trentino heatedly. "Sure, we shadow Fire, we shadow him all day." "What day was that?" Chico laughs: "Shadowday. Some joke, huh, boss?" Harpo meanwhile has been giving his attention to Trentino, cutting the tails off his coat (Gottlieb's evening coat attracts him similarly at the end of *A Night at the Opera*). He smears paste on the seat of Trentino's trousers and, shaking hands with him as he leaves, closes a mousetrap on his fingers. As Trentino leans back on his desk. he affixes a newspaper to his pants, having been only a little less vigorously dealt with than Miss Marlowe will be in *A Day at the Races*.

Harpo has a positive mania for cutting things. There's Trentino's cigar, Chico's sausage, and Zeppo's hat after he has passed Harpo in a corridor. Zeppo looks quite bewildered, as well he might, when he finds only half of it left on his head but his reactions are those of a complete outsider, not a Marx brother. (Groucho might well be fooled by Harpo but he never looks quite so baffled — he'd know *who* had done it if not *how*).

Old tricks of Harpo appear, like his handing Chico his leg or starting a fight, threatening a punch and delivering a kick. In this scrap, Harpo gets involved with the queue at a lemonade seller's cart. The man rightly grows indignant at this disturbance to his business. Chico demonstrates how Harpo has been kicking him by kicking the Lemonade Seller while Harpo stands around smiling and eventually gives him his leg. The man advances menacingly on Harpo and collides with him. Their hats fall off and they pick up the wrong ones. There is a smoothly played sequence with all three of them exchanging hats and ending up with the wrong one. This was probably a *forte* of vaudeville and it is interesting that it turns up in Samuel Beckett's *Waiting for Godot*. One wonders where Beckett saw it; certainly the Marx Brothers have had their influence on writers like Beckett.

The Lemonade Seller is reduced to such a state that he gives Harpo his leg and Chico gives the man one of *his* legs In other words, he doesn't know who he is (the 'loss of individuality' theme once more). But underlying this scene is the feeling that this is rather crude knockabout and, more importantly, that the Lemonade Seller hasn't provoked Chico or Harpo in any way.

When later the man takes a packet of peanuts from Harpo and refuses to pay for it, he deserves all he gets and we can enjoy it that much more. The man overturns the peanut stand and Harpo responds by rolling up his trousers and paddling gleefully in the man's glass container of lemonade. This is a powerful image as we can identify

DUCK SOUP: As Harpo and Chico break into the Teasdale mansion,
Groucho informs the worried Mrs. Teasdale (Margaret Dumont)
that it's mice who are making all the noise downstairs.

with Harpo's right to avenge himself and his childish pleasure in
churning up the lemonade, but our standards of hygiene mean that
we recoil at the idea of dirty feet despoiling a liquid that came so
close to human consumption. It is both satisfying and horrifying: an
unforgettable image (among many) of a Marx brother at work. It
is an updating, too, of the Robin Goodfellow or Puck of medieval
times whose delights included dancing in the butter churns.

The Lemonade Seller is perhaps fair game for another encounter
with Harpo but the circumstances rate him a little sympathy at
least. Harpo is doing a Paul Revere act, riding around alerting the
people to the war that has been declared. He spies a woman undress-
ing in her bedroom and, after seeing that his horse is well nourished
(again the concern for horses), goes in after a form of nourishment
himself. He is seen lying on the bed just as she spots her husband
returning. He is the Lemonade Seller. Harpo hides in the bathroom
and the man asks for what happens by refusing to be a patriot and
set out to fight. No, he's going to take a bath, and it is here that we
have the crushing form of humour again as he settles down in his
bath water on top of Harpo.

Duck Soup further develops Harpo's love for horses. He eventually reaches his own house where a woman is waving to him from a
window. It is late at night and the camera tracks along the foot of a
bed showing a pair of high-heeled shoes, Harpo's boots, and a set of
horseshoes, all neatly laid out. Then in the shot that follows this, we

89

see Harpo's order of priorities established: the three are asleep but it is Harpo and the horse that share the double bed while the woman has been consigned to a single bed in the corner.

In this film, Harpo is much more human than in his two preceding appearances. Such moments as his discomfort when lemonade has been poured into his trousers by the Lemonade Seller (his rueful expression admits that the man temporarily outwitted him as he wriggles about) or his reluctance to be a volunteer (when Chico's crooked method of selection picks him out) are ones that let us react to Harpo as a creature of feelings that are almost human.

* * *

DUCK SOUP: Chico turns his trial into a sideshow encouraged by Groucho.

Harpo also takes pleasure in outwitting Groucho. Throughout the film Groucho never succeeds in being taken anywhere by his chauffeur, Harpo, who always leaves without him, even when he is smart enough to take the driving seat himself. Nothing is beyond Harpo as Groucho discovers when he takes an interest in the blonde Harpo has tattooed on his arm. He has her 'phone number all right, on another area of skin. He has his home, a dog kennel, from which — as Groucho peers closely — a real dog emerges to bark at him (superb special effects: it does not look faked at all and we can laugh unreservedly). "I suppose you haven't got a picture of my grandfather?" asks Groucho. Harpo grins and nods: he's got everything.

Harpo's *tour de force* in outsmarting Groucho comes with his impersonation of his brother. With Chico, he has entered Mrs. Teasdale's home late at night, looking for Freedonia's war plans. They hear that Groucho is coming over and, independent of each other, alight on the same idea and dress up in white nightshirts and nightcaps, adding Groucho's moustache, eyebrows, and a cigar. The Marxes are not that similar in appearance. Groucho's face is lean whereas Chico's is fuller and Harpo's is round. Yet the likeness is quite extraordinary. The white of their costumes gives them a kind of ghostly, ethereal quality. Not that they are exactly fleeting in their progress through the house: Harpo gallops eagerly along the corridor on his way to fool Mrs Teasdale and slithers perilously in his socks at the foot of the stairs. He also runs headlong into a mirror instead of passing through it. Conveniently, however, the broken glass vanishes and a room is revealed beyond the mirror. Like the absence of the puppet master in *Monkey Business* this does not matter but it would have been neater still for Harpo just to stand in a doorway without there having been any mirror when Groucho comes along and Harpo is forced to pose as his reflection.

DUCK SOUP: A musical celebration of the advent of war with the four Marxes and government officials of Freedonia.

Groucho suspects his 'reflection' and makes some elaborate tests — wiggling his behind, poking his head around the edge of the frame, doing strange dances back and forth — but he can't fool the image. Now the obvious solution would be to feel and see if the mirror was there; but Groucho knows the rules. He has to play the game and outwit Harpo legitimately. At one point they actually circle round one another and thereby change sides but this makes no difference. Harpo doesn't entirely imitate Groucho — when Groucho whirls around quickly, he economises on effort by merely matching a hopeful Groucho when the latter ends up facing him and throws out his hands.

At one point Harpo accidentally drops the hat he is holding and Groucho obligingly reaches out and hands it back to him, allowing him the lapse. Harpo's motions have caught the spirit of Groucho, but now his own personality seeks to be released and his face lapses into a grin at one moment, only to stiffen sharply. For him, as for Groucho, it is a game. It could continue indefinitely but for Chico arriving on the scene in his Groucho disguise. Seeing two 'reflections' gives the game to Groucho and he rushes through to seize Chico by his nightshirt. Earlier, in a moment of unparalleled intelligence and foresight, he had Freedonian troops surround the house and this is presumably how he restrains his Minister of War although Harpo escapes.

* * *

Chico obtains his job after Groucho calls him away from his peanut stall. As Chico arrives, the telephone rings and Chico answers it. Despite the fact that Groucho is in the room, Chico tells the caller

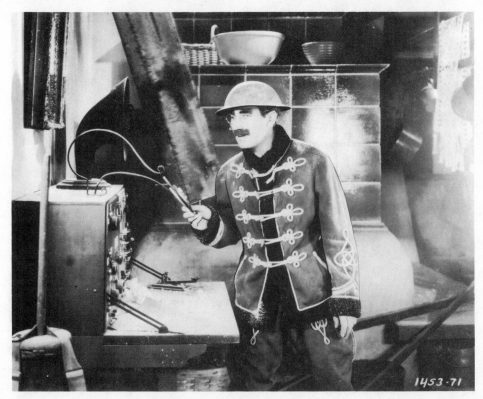

1453·71

that he isn't. This happens again and Groucho looks around, saying: "I wonder whatever became of me." Here, too, as in the multiplicity of Grouchos in Mrs. Teasdale's house, there is the recurrent theme of attack on the individual for, if he can be so easily multiplied or so completely overlooked, what individual existence does he have? Groucho is really fighting with the mirror Groucho to regain his individuality by proving to himself that it is different from him. If Harpo can go on matching him, then Harpo can go on being Groucho forever.

Groucho and Chico involve each other in some childish quizzing, started by Groucho and won by Chico in a decisive countermove. Groucho has what he, as a national leader, regards as a "very important question": "What is it that has four pair of pants, lives in Philadelphia, and it never rains but it pours?" Groucho chuckles gleefully in the expectation of having baffled Chico when the latter says: "That's a good question. I give you three guesses." Groucho then tries a couple of questions before giving up. Chico gives up, too. They have reached a totally inglorious deadlock. There is nothing more to be said and no point found in having said what has been said. It is more than enough to make sages despair and the monkeys laugh.

Somewhat similar is an arabesque of elaborate pointlessness performed by Chico and Harpo in their attempts to slip inside the Teasdale mansion. They ring the bell and hide behind a privet hedge as the footman comes out and looks around. The pair run out and Harpo dashes inside to shut the door on Chico. Then Chico rings the bell and Harpo comes out and has the door shut on him by Chico. He knocks on the door and Chico comes out. They hear the footman coming back so both hide behind the hedge as he goes in and shuts the door. Both have been inside the house. Both are now outside — like Groucho and Chico locked out of the speakeasy in *Horse Feathers*. Somehow the simple use of a door defeats them. Yet the Marxes' pleasure always lies in doing or saying things rather than what is achieved by it.

Groucho tells Chico that he can't have the job he was going to be offered. "What job was that?" "Secretary of War," answers Groucho. "Good, I take it," replies Chico. "Sold!" cries Groucho. Therefore Chico gets the position after having been explicitly deprived of it and Groucho completely contradicts what he said a moment before. The words are plain enough but they don't have their commonly accepted meanings; yet without these meanings, man's basic achievement of communication is quite lost. In court Groucho asks Chico: "Think of a number from one to ten." "Eleven," replies Chico. "Right!" declares Groucho. English has suddenly become a foreign language, or a language with its meanings reversed.

Chico also puts his listeners on trial in court by subjecting them

DUCK SOUP:
Groucho radios for
help in Freedonia's   93
hour of need.

to some of his most far-fetched puns and worsening his chances. Groucho makes the mistake of referring to him as "an abject figure". "I abject!" cries Chico. Here we must credit Groucho with outwitting Chico at least once. He carries on, saying: "I say look at Chicolini — there he sits, a pitiable object — let's see you get out of that one — surrounded by a sea of unfriendly faces." Chico remains silent.

* * *

Duck Soup is the most lavish of the Paramount films, as is clear from the huge sets of the inauguration ceremony and the courthouse and by the large numbers (if partly matte work) that appear in them. When hostilities are declared, there is a spectacular musical ensemble led by the four Marxes *celebrating* the advent of war, which goes through a number of musical styles, among them the negro spiritual ('All God's chillun got guns' — an almost blasphemous idea), the hillbilly song ('Comin' Round the Mountain') and the barn-dance. It ends with Harpo's being despatched to arouse the citizenry.

The climax continues on the battlefield. Groucho orders a message to be sent. "Is there any answer to the message?" he asks the radio operator. There isn't. "In that case don't send it," he adds. Like Chico in their next film ("You pay him enough he could sail yesterday") Groucho doesn't accept the finality of time and the limitation it imposes on logic. Groucho's costume changes, too, in a kind of retrospective survey of military uniforms (so that his actions

DUCK SOUP: The Marxes' last stand — but victory is just around the corner.

do not apply just to one period), and the war becomes nothing more than a mad game in which the ultimate weapon that brings the enemy to surrender is not an atom bomb but hard cooking apples.

Chico turns up belatedly with an answer to Freedonia's defeats: he's joined the other side. He's only come back because the food is better on the Freedonian side. Shells keep flying across the room and Groucho darts over to pull down the blind and keep them out. He loses his rifle through the window and turns to Margaret Dumont: "Run out and get it for me like a good girl." He also has a vase stuck on his head which brings out another glimpse of the thwarted Casanova: "The last time this happened to me I was crawling under a bed." Harpo dislodges the vase by lighting a stick of dynamite and inserting it in a gap.

In other words, war has become an absurd farce: without meaning, without logic. When Groucho declares: "But there must be a war — I've paid a month's rent on the battlefield", he is accurately parodying the politicians who have gone into war from some trivial consideration of pride and self-justification. The end of *Duck Soup* is a comment on all wars: that they are pointless, tending to arise from trivialities, to be rejoiced in by men as a kind of super-game, and won by chance and luck. Margaret Dumont tries to instil glory into the victory by undertaking the National Anthem but the Marx brothers won't have any such gooey notion spoiling the sheer fun of it and shower her with the remaining apples. The film's implications are pacifist and it may be of interest to recall that *Duck Soup* was banned in the Italy of Mussolini.

Duck Soup is the most highly regarded of the Marxes' pictures. Groucho himself thinks it the craziest. If such a thing were strictly calculable, *Duck Soup* would probably turn out to have the greatest density and penetration of wit, partly because it has the good sense to stick to the essentials. Much of *A Night at the Opera* has faded a bit because it was geared for contemporary tastes, but *Duck Soup* is almost mint-fresh today and will be timelessly funny. There is no boring sideline romance; there is no respite (though perhaps there should be) for Harpo and Chico to perform on harp and piano (contrary to what is often said, not even on first release did the film contain their usual specialities); and there are scarcely any plot scenes. Leo McCarey may let several little discrepancies through (jumps from long shot to close-up that do not match, etc.) but he has a solid grip on the film as a whole and — without changing them — on the Marx Brothers too.

McCarey's own reminiscences [33] confirm the difficulties of working with men who were as troublesome off-screen as they are to the other characters on-screen. Perhaps as a result he shows a surprising lack of affection for the film, and perhaps he was able to impose too little of himself on their set image.

8. A Night at the Opera (1935)

Executive-level changes at Paramount and the unexciting box-office performance of *Duck Soup* eventually led the Marx Brothers to Irving G. Thalberg at M-G-M. It was Chico who here, as on other occasions, set up the deal from the Marx side (Zeppo dropping out to become their agent). Both *A Night at the Opera* and *A Day at the Races* stemmed from this collaboration with Thalberg who went to the expense of letting the team test their key scenes in front of audiences to get them into the best shape for filming. He also agreed to let Kaufman and Ryskind write the script and for this reason it has many outstanding scenes. At other moments, Thalberg's ideas for widening the team's appeal come into play: there is a rather lamentable softening of their characters and they defer too much to the plot. They also stand aside for a rather trite (if pleasantly acted) romance and some elaborate musical numbers, both providing contrast with the comedy. This takes one back to Kaufman and Ryskind's script for *The Cocoanuts* which was also 'well-balanced' in much the same way; and here, as there, one can concentrate on the Marx scenes and largely ignore the rest. Thalberg's judgement was shrewd: both his Marx pictures did excellent business in the theatres.

A NIGHT AT THE OPERA: "Well, you see the spaghetti, don't you?" Groucho, as Otis B. Driftwood, tries to point out Hermann Gottlieb to Margaret Dumont as Mrs. Claypool.

The opening scene, set in a restaurant in Milan, is superb. Margaret Dumont, as Mrs. Claypool, has been 'stood up' by Groucho, as Otis B. Driftwood. To make matters worse, she finds he has been dining with a blonde, not just in the same restaurant but directly behind her. Groucho has no trouble dealing with both women: the blonde he leaves with the check (and the following advice: "$ 9.40! This is an outrage! If I were you I wouldn't pay it"), while Margaret Dumont he comforts with a jovial slap on the back and the wildest possible flattery — that he was only sitting with the blonde because of the likeness to her. Furthermore, adds Groucho, "That's why I'm sitting here with you. Because you remind me of you. Your eyes, your throat, your lips... everything about you reminds me of you. Except you. How do you account for that?" For most people, their appearance is the most distinctive thing about them: in a frontal attack on Margaret Dumont's identity, he asserts that she looks like the blonde and then tells her she doesn't look like herself.

Groucho next introduces Hermann Gottlieb, director of the New York Opera Company, a pompous, bearded figure who obviously stands on ceremony. This is Siegfried Rumann making the first of three splendid appearances in the world of the Marx Brothers, being driven to a frenzy on each occasion. Promptly testing the man's patience and the power of etiquette, Groucho has Gottlieb and Mrs. Claypool and himself repeatedly bowing to each other, stretching such formal introductions to absurdity. No sooner has Gottlieb kissed Mrs. Claypool's hand than Groucho imputes dishonesty to men of his appearance and manner by checking her rings. In *A Day at the Races* Rumann plays a stiff-backed Viennese doctor with a goatee and Groucho prefers to keep his watch on while rinsing his hands rather than leave it within reach of such a man.

Gottlieb is warned that making love to Mrs. Claypool is Groucho's "racket" but is then generously allowed to "take a whack at it" — as though it were some kind of sport anyone can try on her. Groucho merely reminds him that he saw her first; then, ever the stickler for unhelpful accuracy, he corrects himself: "Of course, her mother really saw her first but there's no point in bringing the Civil War in-

A NIGHT AT
THE OPERA:
The contract scene,
Chico and Groucho
negotiate back stage
at the opera.

A NIGHT AT
THE OPERA:
Groucho finds the
three stowaways
in his luggage: Allan
Jones as Ricardo,
Harpo and Chico.

to this." Once again Groucho takes a potent phrase, this time about the Civil War, and throws it into the wrong context. This scene also offers a fine example of Groucho's streak of deviousness: he can't just order a glass of milk, he has to have it the hard way. "Have you got any milk-fed chicken?" he asks the waiter and is told yes. "Well, squeeze the milk out of one and bring me a glass."

This scene is finely written to fit Groucho's established character. Its only surprise is that Groucho should actually have arranged the introduction to Gottlieb. It is his job to work her into high society but it would have been more in character had he forced himself and Mrs. Claypool on to Gottlieb on the spur of the moment to prove he had done something to earn his salary.

Gottlieb wants Mrs. Claypool to invest in the Opera Company so that it can afford to bring the famous tenor Rodolpho Lassparri to New York. "You're willing to pay him a thousand dollars a night just for singing?" says Groucho incredulously, adding: "Why, you can buy a phonograph record of Minnie the Moocher for 75c. For a buck and a quarter you can get Minnie!" He slips right to the other extreme by showing that to him singing is singing wherever it's done and whoever does it. But, as always, the money interests Groucho and he sets out to sign up Lassparri and take a cut. With typical incompetence he has forgotten Lassparri's name by the time he encounters Chico backstage at the opera. All Groucho can remember is that he is "the greatest tenor in the world" and so Chico negotiates a contract for his friend Ricardo Baroni whom he regards as fitting Groucho's description.

Leading from this initial mistake (like the one Groucho makes over football players in *Horse Feathers*) is one of the finest Groucho-Chico encounters, as both warily negotiate a contract. "Could he sail to-morrow?" asks Groucho. "You pay him enough money he could sail yesterday," boasts Chico, adding: "How much you pay him?" Groucho ponders a moment. "Well, I don't know... *let's see, a thousand dollars a night... I'm entitled to a small profit...* how about ten dollars a night?" (again swinging to the other extreme). Eventually, after Groucho and Chico have deducted 10% each (unlike

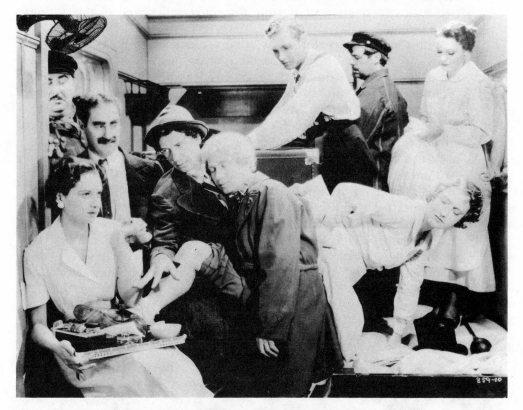

A NIGHT AT THE OPERA: Groucho's minute cabin resembles Times Square in the rush hour, and a drowsy Harpo sprawling around, his foot on offer for the manicurist, doesn't help matters.

later films, Chico isn't so devoted to the hero that he doesn't guard his own interests) and Groucho allows for all the taxes, it transpires that the man can break even as long as he doesn't sing too often. (This is almost as back to front as Chico's explaining in *Animal Crackers* how as a musician he earns most by not playing). Groucho hands him a contract for the singer, a duplicate. Chico chews over the word 'duplicate'; to him that's five kids up in Canada — one of the rare purely topical references (to the Dionne quintets) and a weakness as it will obviously become obscure. Chico can't read the contract, and they launch into one of those slippery exchanges that runs a line of thought right into the ground. "You read it," says

Chico. Groucho: "All right, I'll read it to you. Can you hear?" Chico: "I haven't heard anything yet. Did you say anything?" Groucho: "Well, I haven't said anything worth hearing." Chico: "That's why I didn't hear anything." Groucho: "Well, that's why I didn't say anything." Which takes us to the far end of that cul-de-sac, to a moment of silence for contemplating the foolhardiness of two such characters ever starting the conversation and of our sitting there listening to it.

With Chico as unperturbed as usual, Groucho struggles on and eventually, by tearing off disagreeable clauses, they end up with two mutually acceptable shreds of paper. Groucho offers his fountain pen. "I forgot to tell you," announces Chico, "I can't write." Groucho is not to be outsmarted: "Well, that's all right, there's no ink in the pen anyhow." Harpo couldn't write either in *Horse Feathers* when Groucho offered him a blank piece of paper (a contract with the details to be filled in later). One assumes he can't read, like Chico. Arithmetic is more useful to a smart operator like Chico and he shows a better grasp of this. In later films Chico and Harpo can sometimes read and write as though, with the passage of time, they gained a shaky elementary education.

Groucho quickly finds that for all his trouble in making an agreement, he has failed to sign Lassparri after all, though the man has been right under his feet all the time. Groucho had come along to find the man stretched out cold on the floor and (in a surrealistic

A NIGHT AT THE OPERA: Harpo's tomfoolery at the piano amuses the passengers on the boat.

dislocation of the setting) treated him like a bar-rail, after asking if Chico minds, by saying "Two beers, bartender!" Chico stupidly adds: "I'll take two beers, too."

* * *

Lassparri sails to New York with Gottlieb, Mrs. Claypool, and his leading lady, Rosa, a girl whom Ricardo loves. Groucho manages to get aboard but Gottlieb sees that he has the smallest accommodation available. Once his large travelling trunk is put in, the cabin is even smaller, and Chico and Ricardo soon step out of that leaving Harpo still snoozing in a drawer (like a dog, which is perhaps why he hates other dogs). He collects a further crack from Groucho about his appearance ("as grisly looking an object as I've ever seen"). This develops into another classic scene as a parade of outsiders force their way in on various pretexts ("If she isn't here you can probably find someone just as good", Groucho informs a young lady seeking her aunt, i.e. the run of people are interchangeable, one person is as good as the next). This build-up is given pith by the fact that Groucho is expecting Mrs. Claypool to come along for a quiet *tête-à-tête*. When she arrives and opens the door, she unleashes an avalanche of people into the corridor: a shot that is very convincingly staged. Groucho isn't by tradition a person prone to be thwarted in this way by other people; but the outcome is in line with the romantic assignments broken by Chico and Harpo in later films (and they are part of this one).

The stowaways slip out to eat and mingle with the common folk, the immigrants on the boat. Ricardo sings, his stomach full; Chico amuses the children with his tricky fingerwork. Harpo follows with some tomfoolery at the piano, spinning the seat and letting it rise to meet him (as in *Animal Crackers*), then playing very badly until he can catch one hand under the lid by dashing it down with the other. Much as the whole of his body is limp in the crowded cabin where he flops over the incoming people and plates of food, here first one hand, then the other, refuses to work after being caught in the lid. He dabs them like paintbrushes on the piano, then flaps them over his young audience, who are screaming as merrily at his discomfort as the children watching the Punch and Judy show in *Monkey Business*. Lacking their normal control, these hands are comparable to the 'soft watches' of a Dali painting — an area of contact with the Surrealists. When Harpo feels he has amused them sufficiently, he waits by his harp for silence, then plays. In the shots taken from one angle there is an old woman, whose creased face is meant to typify hardworking European peasant stock, listening attentively. Even though Harpo is now playing for an audience, he chooses simple folk and not the rich passengers. (The same is true in the next three M-G-M films, as he plays twice to poor Negroes, once to primitive Red Indians.) The old lady couldn't afford a seat at the opera, but

A NIGHT AT THE OPERA: Chico and Ricardo coax Harpo into escaping from the brig.

Harpo's music has no price on it (whereas Lassparri contemptuously refuses to sing for nothing to his dockside admirers). Harpo's music is for the poor to sit around and listen to at a suitable moment: they are not obliged to dress up, book seats, and fill an Opera House at a specified time.

Lassparri puts the Captain on the trail of the stowaways and they end up in the brig. Harpo is pushed protestingly through the porthole by Chico (the harsh daylight reflected off the side of the ship produces *too* realistic an effect: the Marx world isn't quite that life-like). Harpo comes across three sleeping celebrities in a nearby cabin; they are bearded aviators. They would have been safe but for the affectation of their beards which constitutes a perfect disguise. Harpo's cutting mania surfaces again and the whiskers are quickly scissored off. (Groucho makes several forays, mostly verbal, at the other beard in the film — that on Gottlieb). Chico, Ricardo and Harpo pose as the aviators at their tickertape welcome. Chico is called on to speak and delivers a full-bodied example of his dense thinking, recalling how he reached America: "The first time we get halfway across when we run out of gasoline and we gotta go back. Then we take twice as much gasoline. This time we were just about to land — maybe three feet — when what do you think? We run out of gasoline again and back we go again to get-a more gasoline." Like "If you pay him enough, he could sail yesterday", Chico is logical in a way that ignores the practical limitations. He continues: "This time plenty gas.

Then I get a great idea. We no take-a gasoline. We take a steamship! And that, friends, is how we fly across the ocean." As when Chico tells a departing guest the train schedules in *The Cocoanuts* ("Train? Once a week, sometimes twice a day"), the world is too polite a place to question an authoritative assertion, however baffling.

Later, Kaufman and Ryskind, who made such a feature of Harpo's appetite in *The Cocoanuts,* revive it spectacularly here as Harpo breakfasts in Groucho's apartment on a cigar sandwich and a tie placed between hotcakes. "He's half goat," declares Chico, which suggests Harpo as Pan. A moment later, yet another suspicious offi-

A NIGHT AT THE OPERA: Harpo, Ricardo, and Chico make their first appearance masquerading as the bearded aviators to leave the ship for the big welcome.

cial enters the Marx world, a detective seeking the stowaways who deceived everyone as aviators, and despite all his wariness, fares as badly as the others. The rooms seem to rearrange themselves behind his back as Harpo and Chico slip out of hiding while Groucho gives a conducted tour and verbally chisels into his wavering composure. This ends with the sublime glimpse of Harpo, his face puffed out in a 'gookie' and a tea cosy on his head, rocking in an armchair that is really Chico covered with a sheet, while Groucho sits nearby wearing an impenetrable false beard — a sight that makes the man think he wandered into the wrong room and retire hopelessly defeated.

*   *   *

Soon after this, it is the Marxes who face defeat, along with the two people they care about. Groucho is subtly weakened in this film as before this his competence was never questioned; here Gottlieb gains Mrs. Claypool's confidence and has him sacked as a fraud. This occurs in an elaborate sequence with everyone conspiring to welcome him in (he himself unsuspectingly reciprocates their greetings — he *can* be at peace with the world), then helping to boot him out. He can't even get a seat in the park. "I'd give you my seat but I'm sitting here," says Chico, self-interest first as always. Groucho can't sit on the grass without being ordered off, and the water fountain mysteriously dries up on him (fate is his enemy, as in the cabin scene). Rosa, Ricardo's girl friend, has lost her job as leading lady

A NIGHT AT THE OPERA: The three Marxes and Ricardo invade the offices of Gottlieb, and Harpo prepares to knock out the impresario as he attempts to phone the police and have them arrested.

A NIGHT AT THE OPERA: Groucho makes off to the adjacent box at the opera house as an enraged Gottlieb arrives, having been locked up by the Marxes and reduced to wearing Groucho's clothes.

at Lassparri's intervention, for not being in love with him. Chico is concerned through his liking for Ricardo, and Groucho has also shown an interest in Rosa, running a message from Ricardo when she thinks the boat has sailed without him and being captivated by a rewarding kiss. Lassparri, of course, had the stowaways locked up on the boat, and Harpo knows him as a mean bully, having been whipped (despite pleading child-like for a truce) for wearing some of his costumes and beaten up as the man works off a polite rebuff from Rosa.

So now the three Marx brothers and the two romantic leads have all reached the depths of despair in the park. This degree of concern for others and this vulnerability to misfortune are quite new to the Marx Brothers. Facing charges for impersonating the aviators, they actually offer to give themselves up if Gottlieb will reinstate Rosa as the leading lady. Gottlieb refuses. All this humiliation has the effect of making the Marx Brothers more sympathetic, and it is an established fact that women filmgoers (notoriously resistant to the team prior to this) want to be able to respond to the good characters on the screen, perhaps to imagine domesticating them. Mary McCarthy overheard a woman's criticism of Jimmy Porter in *Look*

A NIGHT AT THE OPERA: Harpo joins the musicians at the opera.

Back in Anger as "He wouldn't let me pity him." The Marx Brothers also asked nothing from their audience until Thalberg got hold of them; and like Jimmy Porter they don't allow themselves to be tamed. Of course, it is also classic plot construction to reduce them to near hopelessness so that their subsequent triumph is the greater as is the pleasure the audience draws from siding with them. But it does make them more predictable. Before this, one did not really have preconceptions in a Marx picture; one sat back not knowing what would happen next. The new formula offers the contradiction of displaying form and logic, two qualities that Marx humour itself scarcely accepts, but it is this that makes *A Night at the Opera* more accessible to general audiences.

Thus Gottlieb, Lassparri and the entire Opera House merit their fate. The attack is not on opera itself, to which the Marxes are quite indifferent. (Groucho is seen earlier arriving at the very end of a performance, making sure he doesn't hear a note.) Once Ricardo and Rosa are performing, peace and quiet reigns and the audience is grateful to the Marxes for having unexpectedly improved the quality of the performance by removing Lassparri. They are responding to provocation in their attack on the opera.

The climax brilliantly exploits the basic factor in comedy, that of incongruity. The civilised atmosphere is rent by Groucho yelling

A NIGHT AT
THE OPERA:
Harpo and Chico
start a fencing match
with violin bows in
the orchestra pit.

"Peanuts! Peanuts!" and by Chico and Harpo inserting 'Take Me Out to the Ball Game' in the overture scores so that, after a carefully timed build-up, all the pages turn and the orchestra launch into the number. There is nothing wrong with peanuts or popular music except in this particular context. Later we see the incongruity of the opera singers performing in front of changing backcloths: a railway yard, fruit stalls and a battleship behind the performers make them look suddenly and simply ridiculous. Gottlieb and the policeman creep on stage in ill-fitting gypsy costumes, grotesque and grim. The Marxes enjoy themselves, especially Harpo who enthusiastically makes faces, waves to the audience from the stage, rips off the costume of a passing dancer, and clambers up the backcloth to escape the police who are swarming in each wing. Things grow worse and worse until the theatre goes pitch-black and Lassparri's voice is choked off as the Marxes kidnap him. When he eventually returns on stage, he quickly hurries off again to a chorus of booing, and expostulates: "They threw an apple at me!" "Well, water melons are out of season," says Groucho, a fund of useless knowledge (his sagacity is always superficial; he doesn't believe in real scholarship). Gottlieb isn't clear of trouble when he accepts Rosa and Ricardo for he has to negotiate a contract with two such skilled negotiators as Chico and Groucho while Harpo playfully splits his evening coat up the back and cuddles close to him as he looks around, smiling seraphically upwards at him.

* * *

A Night at the Opera is both a master product of the Hollywood assembly line (director Sam Wood deserves credit for his staging of the film) and a vehicle for the highly distinctive personalities of the

Marx Brothers. Whether the changes this involved in the team's character enhance or diminish this film is a matter of personal preference. For many it is the best of their work; few will hold it in less than high esteem.

A NIGHT AT THE OPERA: The farewell shot — Groucho and Chico negotiate new contracts with Gottlieb as Harpo playfully splits the back of his evening dress.

9. A Day at the Races (1937)

While it gives considerable satisfaction to most Marx enthusiasts, *A Day at the Races* is a lesser achievement than *A Night at the Opera*. Thalberg died after it had gone into production but as his contribution lay mostly in the pre-planning and organisation of the picture, this unhappy event cannot have greatly altered the finished product. Again they were allowed to make a road tour testing material. Again they were backed up by top talent (including Sam Wood to direct them once more) and by a lavish budget. However, there is a certain forced quality about the film, obviously in part through new writers being used. Despite several innovations in the pattern of Marx comedy (repeated in later films), it feels a little repetitive and unadventurous as though a formula is at work. In small ways, the script is undermining the team.

* * *

"I'm going to someone who understands me. I'm going to Dr. Hackenbush! Why, I never knew there was a thing the matter with me until I met him!" Thus cries Margaret Dumont as Mrs. Emily Upjohn,. indignant at the sanitarium doctors' refusal to find anything wrong with her. One doesn't need telling who Dr. Hackenbush must be and Margaret Dumont's blind faith in Groucho against all other medical opinion is very promising, especially when it transpires that her physician, who always made such a point of treating her in the home, is in fact a horse doctor. (Back in *Monkey Business* Groucho posed as a doctor when a man fainted and rushed up asking: "Where's the horse?") A loan from Mrs. Upjohn is the only hope of keeping the sanitarium from closing down. Chico, who is devoted to its pretty young owner, Judy Standish, declares that "If she wants a Hackenabuss, she's gonna get a Hackenabuss", and so Groucho is summoned posthaste to assure Mrs. Upjohn that she really is ill. He leaves what appears to be an active business as a veterinarian; it is a strange idea that he should have ever settled down to anything, particularly as skilled as this. He is an even more conventional figure at the end when he makes a genuine proposal to Emily: "Marry me and I'll never look at any other horse." It is at least a logical extension of Groucho's history of likening Margaret Dumont to various animals. While it may be a happy ending for the average spectator, we can put it down to a temporary aberration that Groucho will wriggle out of later.

"Ah, Emily, she never forgot that hayride," says Groucho on receiving Chico's telegram, conjuring up a rich image of the pair under a harvest moon. "He's here! He's here!" she cries as he stalks in, and her touching faith doesn't waver when he goes on to treat her like any of his other patients. He hands her a gigantic horse-pill and reassures her: "You have nothing to worry about. The last patient I gave one of those won the Kentucky Derby." Not even an expert from Vienna, Dr. Leopold X. Steinberg, who promptly declares he has never heard of an ailment called double blood pressure, can shake her belief. While Groucho stands apprehensively to one side, his eyeballs darting from one side to the other like the confused corpuscles he has detected in Mrs. Upjohn, she proudly relates, "Dr. Hackenbush tells me I'm the only case in history. I have *high* blood pressure on my right side and *low* blood pressure on my left side!"

Groucho has to forestall several attempts to check on his credentials made by Whitmore, the sanitarium's financial adviser. Mrs. Upjohn does touch Groucho gently on the shoulder and scold him for being sharp with Whitmore but the man rates no sympathy because we know he is trying to get the sanitarium closed so that a big operator, Morgan, can redevelop it as a gambling casino to go with his nearby racetrack. Whitmore probes Groucho's medical background and has him admitting that medically his experiences have been most

A DAY AT THE RACES: "Tutsi-frutsi ice-cream." Chico gives a helping hand to the sucker (Groucho) that he has found at the racetrack.

unexciting "except during the 'flu epidemic." On saying this Groucho drops into a tense pose, leaning forward and looking straight ahead waiting for the signal to deliver his punchline. "Ah, and what happened?" asks Whitmore obligingly. "I got the 'flu," answers Groucho. Later, on learning of Whitmore's plan to 'phone the Florida Medical Board and check up that way, Groucho handles the man brilliantly. He does exaggerated voice impersonations of the receptionists at both ends of the line, as well as of a Colonel Hawkins of the Florida Medical Board, in elaborately faking the call. By having the southern-twanged Colonel half-deaf and simulating a hurricane with paper rustled in the electric fan, he drives Whitmore into a frenzy of shouting into the telephone. He then buzzes Whitmore on the intercom system in his own voice and tells him his shouting is annoying the patients. Thus he has neatly placed the man in a crossfire between Hackenbush and Hawkins. It should be noted that Groucho's moves are entirely aggressive and not at all constructive: instead of allaying Whitmore's suspicions by giving himself a respectable background he works on the man's short temper, having taken an instinctive but later justified dislike for the man, and leaves him even keener to catch Hackenbush out in the future. Groucho lives entirely for the moment.

The big test comes when Mrs. Upjohn agrees to be examined by both doctors. Groucho has but one instinct: to run. However, since he has also the welfare of the heroine at heart, Chico easily persuades him to bluff it out with Steinberg. Earlier Groucho has hinted at his deception to Judy Standish, looking down and fidgeting with his fingers. She says that, whatever he might turn out to be, he's her only hope — which makes it all right for him to go on. The old Groucho, of course, would have shown no such signs of loyalty and conscience. He even uses a romantic scene with Mrs. Upjohn to encourage her to make Judy the loan. This type of weakness occurred in *A Night at the Opera* but not to this extent nor so early, and this weakens Groucho's performance. The Paramount films would also not have had anyone seeing through Groucho's façade as Whitmore does (the other doctors say nothing but their jobs might be threatened if they spoke out). But then this is also the first time that he has been a deliberate fraud — before this, he has been incompetent but people have accepted him for what he is, or deceived themselves about him, never *been* deceived or misled by him.

Chico is even more concerned about Judy's predicament than Groucho. He is so loyal that he will continue working for her even if she cannot pay him. He it is who tries to get everybody smiling again when things are at their darkest. Whereas Chico has until now been living in a mental twilight, he emerges from it to be a lot smarter in this and in *Go West*, and any stupidity (as at the start of *Go West*) is largely a pretence.

The traditional Chico-Groucho encounter is here an elaborate seven-minute sequence, beautifully played out, in which Groucho is a complete sucker who is methodically fleeced by Chico (all he hands back is a couple of insults) and ends up buying a completely useless racing tip. Having accepted the original tip, Groucho has to buy a succession of books to decode it. He catches on, but too late, and goes through with it to the bitter end, finding he has a losing horse in a finished race while the animal he was going to back has won. The image of Groucho, anchored to the ground, books stuffed between his legs and under his arms, darkly eyeing Chico while the latter walks up and down with his "tutsi-frutsi ice-cream" cart waiting for Groucho to initiate the next round, is a memorable summation of Groucho's experience with Chico.

Harpo is a jockey at the racetrack and a friend of Chico. They run to meet each other but whereas in *A Night at the Opera* this led to the rather touching discovery that they have brought each other (identical) presents, here Harpo's petty dishonesty wins and he darts past Chico to raid his ice-cream cart. Their friendship provides one of the firm links between racetrack and sanitarium like the opening scene at the station and the interest Judy's boy friend, Gil Stewart, has in horses. Harpo starts by working for the villain, Morgan, but is fired for not throwing a race — he gets kicked, which corresponds to the whipping he received from Lassparri in the previous film. Here, though, he is allowed to get his own back in a man-

A DAY AT THE RACES: When Mrs. Upjohn agrees to an independent medical examination, Groucho's instinct is to pack his bags and run. Chico, aided by Gil (Allan Jones) and Harpo, persuades him to stay.

ner that also indicates how much (and this later proves to be important) Gil's horse, Hi-Hat, hates Morgan. Dishonesty in Harpo is confined to small matters, like taking care of the sheriff who tries to collect money owing in stable fees, Chico produces a banknote at a time, with Harpo busily reclaiming it from the sheriff's pocket and passing it back to Chico to hand over again. Later, when the man tries to impound Gil's horse, it takes Harpo, impishly substituting himself for the horse after the man leads it away, to save the situation. (Harpo likens himself to a horse, and thus reaffirms his close relation with this type of animal.)

Even before Chico finds out about Groucho's secret, he brings Harpo into the sanitarium to keep an eye on things. Harpo is to be registered as a patient and has one of his best opportunities while being medically examined by Groucho. (Despite his prominence in the climax, Harpo doesn't have a great deal to do.) Having earlier demonstrated his lack of dedication (making off to the racetrack) and his laziness (riding a wheelchair to his desk), Groucho goes on to display his utter incompetence as any kind of physician. He tries taking Harpo's pulse, looks at his watch, and presents an entertaining alternative: "Either this man is dead or my watch has stopped." Harpo is far from happy at Groucho's work and tootles on a flute looking very nervous as Chico, though he knows Groucho was a sucker for his racing tip, expresses a belief in him as a doctor. Groucho taps at Harpo's knees and inspects his legs, allowing Harpo to clamber on his back. Groucho regains his feet and sticks a thermometer into Harpo's mouth. Harpo calmly chews his way through it like a stick of candy, then washes it down with a bottle of poison. Groucho then looks more closely at Harpo through an auriscope fastened around his head. After making a very gloomy diagnosis, Chico points out that he has been looking at the mirror's reflection of himself, not at Harpo. Groucho prances around childishly pretending it was all a joke on his part, Harpo blankly provides a flute accompaniment, and Chico now looks distinctly unimpressed. (Contrasting with his gaffes in *Horse Feathers* and *Duck Soup*, it is proper for him to lose face here, as his only audience is his brothers who

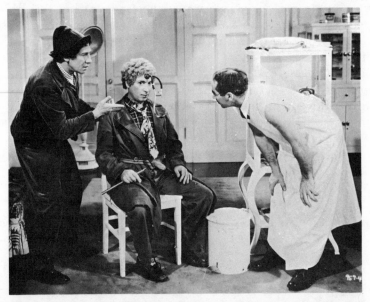

A DAY AT THE RACES: Back at the sanitarium. Chico explains about his friend Harpo to Doctor Hackenbush, i.e. Groucho.

always have the upper hand with him.) Groucho carries on, pressing Harpo's chest. A balloon pops out of his mouth and inflates. By gripping Harpo around the neck, Chico is able to keep the balloon out while Groucho looks for an instrument to examine it more closely. Harpo leans forward and Groucho takes his head as the strange growth which he observes is now covered by red fungus. Corrected again by Chico, Groucho makes a stronger comeback by declaring that, if it *is* Harpo's head, then he's the one that should worry. After Chico stumbles on evidence of Groucho's horse-doctoring past, Groucho comes clean. "I haven't got a leg to stand on," he declares as Harpo injects his leg with an anaesthetic and it goes as stiff as a board, collapsing beneath him. He struggles awkwardly out of the room while Chico and Harpo follow in an imitative walk, one leg stiff, the other wrapped around it. This would be nasty if it copied a genuine disability (as other comedians have) but the Marxes' work is remarkably free of such shortcomings. As we look on this complete routing of Groucho, he earns from us a little commiseration for his troubles, faced with exposure whether he does or doesn't stick with Judy. But there is no demand for sympathy and this is another strength of the team.

Groucho's next encounter with the pair comes as he starts his dinner date with Miss Marlowe, a lanky blonde hired by Whitmore to lure him into a compromising position. Harpo overhears this trap being arranged and tells Chico in the first of their mimed-message scenes. This one is short and simple, Harpo whistling with the fingers of his left hand to comment on Chico's guesses, keeping the other hand free to shake with him when he's right. Harpo first places a finger across his upper lip and lopes up and down but Chico only guesses Hackenbush when Harpo hacks at a bush. Harpo then describes a vertically undulating shape to indicate — a snake? (no) an apple dumpling? (no). Harpo dismisses Chico's guesses and tries pulling up a trouser leg to show flesh. A woman? Yes. Harpo stamps his feet and pretends to knock. Chico is slow to catch on and Harpo raps his brow in exasperation. A headache? Chico eventually guesses a knock on a door. Then Harpo takes a park sign off a tree and knocks it out of its frame. As Harpo waves the frame at him, Chico eventually gets the word 'frame'. Harpo collapses from sheer exhaustion at the effort as Chico pieces the message together and drags him off to rescue Groucho.

Groucho is cutting a wonderfully absurd figure, preening himself in the mirror, spraying the air as he dances around to a Strauss waltz, tidying the flowers on the table, showing all the anxieties of an adolescent on a first big date as he waits for Miss Marlowe. But, once she arrives, through ineptitude and deep-seated traits of character, he constantly punctures this extravagantly romantic image. He carefully seats her and slips on to his own chair without taking his eyes

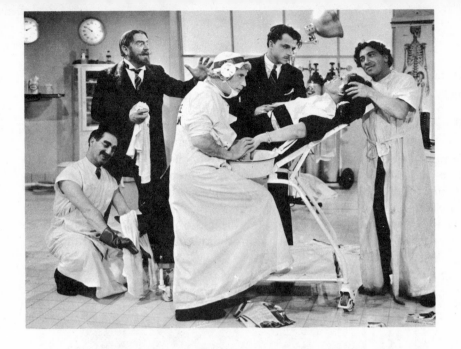

A DAY AT THE RACES: Getting to work on Margaret Dumont. A manicure, a shoe shine and a quick shave leave Dr. Steinberg looking aghast and Whitmore looking sympathetic. Below: other developments. Left, the three doctors insist on cleanliness. Right, Harpo mistakes "X ray" for "Extra!"

off her so that it goes over, spilling him on to the floor (a second time it rocks precariously but he just manages to keep his balance). She has only to inquire, "Oh, how about a little Scotch?" for Groucho to hold out his glass expectantly (the reversal of roles popping up again). "Tomato soup?" he soon asks and takes a tin out of the soup bowl, wondering if she carries a can opener.

Harpo and Chico do their best to break up this romantic idyll. They leap on her lap, Harpo eagerly beckoning Groucho to join them. Then, pulling on one arm as Groucho holds the other, they threaten to tear her asunder in the most glaring of the Marxes' attacks on identity (which comes from an individual's oneness). She makes up her face after this disturbance and curtly tells Harpo to blow. He blows and face powder settles all over her. Eventually, when Whitmore ushers in Mrs. Upjohn, Miss Marlowe is nowhere to be seen. Chico and Harpo are in the midst of redecorating and Groucho tells her that it will be a honeymoon suite for the two of them, not only foiling Whitmore but for once making capital out of the situation by playing up to Emily yet again. After she has retired, very pleased, Miss Marlowe is allowed out of the depths of the sofa Groucho has been sitting on, like one of the characters crushed by Harpo in earlier films. As she storms out, Harpo wallpapers her rear so that she ends up like Ambassador Trentino in *Duck Soup*. At the close of this scene, the trio have worked together and so it is throughout the rest of the film.

* * *

A DAY AT THE RACES: Paying the stable fees — Chico and Gil stall for time while Harpo fishes for the banknote in the sheriff's pocket to pass it back to Chico.

Firstly, there is the scene in the operating theatre. Chico and Harpo burst in as Groucho's assistants and are properly attired in white except for the words 'Joe's Service Station' and 'Brakes Relined' inscribed on their outfits. They wash hands with Groucho, lustily singing 'Down By the Old Mill Stream', showing once more how one of the ways the Marxes express their solidarity most is in song, with

A DAY AT THE RACES: Groucho protests as Chico takes an interest in his dinner companion, Miss Marlowe (Esther Muir), with Harpo as usual siding with Chico.

Harpo mouthing. They then call for new coats and three nurses bring them in. As Harpo steps forward, arms extended, into the clean outfit, he grasps at the nurse and pulls her outer garments off, leaving her in a slip. Something like this occurs when he leans on the cleaning women in the cabin during *A Night at the Opera* and later when he strips the dancer during the opera.

Margaret Dumont suffers worse indignities here than in any other M-G-M film, except perhaps for being fired from a cannon in *At the Circus*. Harpo slaps shaving lather on her face, Chico starts to scrape it off and Groucho polishes her shoes, then Harpo keeps hitting the handle of the operating chair, bouncing her up and down. Steinberg protests that their methods of examination are absolutely insane and Groucho hits back through medicine's vulnerability for its past mistakes: "Yes, that's what they said about Pasteur!" The doctor, besides taking remarks about his beard, has to tolerate Harpo's wiping his hands on his coat-tails and is pushed back into a basin of water. The overhead sprinklers come on and Gil's racehorse charges through, bringing everything to a riotous adjournment.

Even though Groucho hasn't yet been exposed as a fraud, this fiasco gets them all thrown out. They are at the depths of despair as they dry themselves with Gil around a fire in a barn. This is the clear equivalent of the park scene in *A Night at the Opera*. Groucho tries to take all the blame but becomes indignant when Chico agrees to let him. Judy Standish turns up and makes a brave face. Then she and Gil sing a number 'Tomorrow Is Another Day' that is quite charming and the film starts to brighten up. Harpo attracts the attention of some negro children playing a flute, then adds to his following by popping his head through the windows of various negro shacks. Everywhere he is recognised as Gabriel, bringer of good

news, and it is the first time that Harpo could plausibly be put so far on the side of the angels (quite a switch from the Harpo of *Monkey Business* and *Horse Feathers*, for instance). Groucho and Chico eventually join in the merry-making which is musical and spontaneous (again contrasting with the organisation and ceremony of opera and concert). This atmosphere of abandon is broken by a sharp hand-clap from Morgan and his cronies, Whitmore and the sheriff. This leads to a *mêlée* comparable to the antics in the old barn of *Monkey Business*, and brings to light the fact, unknown to them, that Gil's dud horse, Hi-Hat, is a born jumper. From this discovery comes the climax which is quite inventive and very well staged though with some constructional faults. The Marxes work to delay the big steeplechase until Hi-Hat can be smuggled in (the feed bill is still owing), then retrieved after the sheriff successfully appropriates the horse on a first attempt. What the Marxes do is superficially logical and could really be executed by any set of clowns with much the same success, though it has, of course, distinctive touches.

Hi-Hat eventually manages to enter the race and the Marxes allow it to proceed. Harpo rides Hi-Hat, but without showing very much of a special *rapport* with the animal such as one might expect from his horse-loving past. He needs the help of hearing Morgan's voice (anathema to the animal) to spur Hi-Hat on, and this Groucho and Chico contrive to have relayed over the loudspeakers. But Hi-Hat

A DAY AT THE RACES: Chico and Miss Marlowe.

A DAY AT THE RACES: Harpo leads the Negro children in a musical interlude.

loses, or so it seems, until Harpo realises that in the upset at one jump he and the rider of Morgan's own horse must have exchanged mounts. This little set-back is more than pointless: it puzzles us by coming so late and spoils the flow of the scene; and it deprives Harpo of the glory of riding Hi-Hat over the hardest part of the race, down the home stretch and across the finishing line. The use of Morgan's voice (and earlier, photograph) gives an unfair advantage to Hi-Hat who ought to win by sheer superiority, not by a trick, and certainly not with Morgan's jockey. Also, Judy's rescue of Hi-Hat by staging an accident is a mistake: the sheriff is associated with Morgan and ought to remain a villain pure and simple. Instead he is shown to be very worried by the accident and is duped by his kindheartedness as Gil and Judy steal the horse away from him.

Clearly the formula of the climaxes of *A Night at the Opera* and *A Day at the Races* is the same: the race has been stopped as the opera was stopped; the 'best' horse gets its chance to perform as the best singer did. But the climax of *Opera* is a complete success and this is not. In basic terms, *Opera* has a stronger climax because it is based more firmly on personalities — at stake was a singing career and personal revenge; here it is gaining money to revive a business. Rosa was deprived of her chance through Lassparri's spitefulness, whereas here Judy has taken on a genuine debt. She cancels it from outside (with the steeplechase prize money) whereas she ought to

119

win on her home ground, i.e. by improving business at the sanitarium. Then, in any case, there is a difference in atmosphere between racetrack and opera house, the latter yielding images that are more anarchic, more incongruous. The conceit and pomposity of Gottlieb and Lassparri make them richer targets than a couple of greedy businessmen like Morgan and Whitmore, just as a crowd of opera-going 'snobs' are more deserving than spectators at a racetrack. Thus the climax to *A Night at the Opera* is that much better constructed and that much more awe-inspiring.

Another weakness here is the Water Carnival sequence which is lavish but long and tiresome. It takes attention away from the Marxes for too great a period, and when Chico and Harpo come in at the end, they add their musical numbers which might be better placed in comedy sequences for variety. (Chased by the sheriff, they only perform in this inappropriate setting to stall for time.) Harpo discovers a harp imbedded in the piano, by his uncharacteristically brutal handling of it, but he should have had more reverence for something associated with music and good enough for Chico to play (although in this exclusive setting it might be taken as an attack on highbrow music). The non-Marx Water Carnival numbers are less excusable still when one knows that a Kalmar and Ruby song for Groucho, called 'Dr. Hackenbush', had to be dropped because the film was too long.

*   *   *

Thalberg's death had most regrettable consequences for the Marx Brothers later on. The studio was merely content, for their next two films under the M-G-M contract, to work over the pattern of the first two successes in a careless fashion. Two points make this clear: they were no longer allowed to test their material on the road, and the scriptwriter assigned to the films was not one who had worked with the team previously (nor had any earlier Marx film carried only one name on the writing credit). *At the Circus* shows a clear deterioration but holds up the decline with some excellent scenes, while *Go West* is an ignoble slide to a level of almost complete conventionality. The Marxes become just another comedy team to be shifted into the obvious changing backgrounds. However, the last M-G-M film, *The Big Store*, does mark an attempt to recover the situation. But before these three pictures, the Marxes made something of an experiment at another studio, a version of the play *Room Service*.

10. Room Service (1938)

Room Service, a farce by John Murray and Allen Boretz, opened on Broadway on May 19, 1937, and became a smash hit. It concerned the efforts of a penniless stage producer to keep his cast together in a hotel and get a play staged. RKO Radio paid the then record sum of $ 225,000 for the film rights, having it in mind as a vehicle for the Marx Brothers. Presumably, with the indecision at M-G-M over their future following Thalberg's death, the Marxes had encouraged RKO Radio to line up this outside job. Morrie Ryskind, who had co-authored *The Cocoanuts, Animal Crackers* and *A Night at the Opera*, would seem the ideal choice for the job of adapting the play for the team. Yet a comparison of stage and screen versions shows that surprisingly little change was made. The play was staged on one set representing producer Gordon Miller's room in the White Way Hotel. Ryskind has shifted a little bit of the action. The opening

ROOM SERVICE: Groucho introduces the young playwright to Harpo, "the brains of the organisation."

scene is transferred to the hotel lobby (looking strangely deserted and more fitted to the Alps than New York). One scene is played out in the hotel manager's office. Briefly at the finale we see a first-night audience enjoying the play in the hotel's own theatre. Otherwise, the film is almost entirely confined to two hotel rooms: just occasionally the corridors and the view outside come into the film. We

ROOM SERVICE: Harpo stages the second mock suicide, leaving the irate hotel chief quite horrified.

hardly see other hotel guests and, much more erroneously, never see the actors Miller is so worried about, apart from a few shots of the stage at the very end. *Love Happy* is much more successful in suggesting that there really is a show being put on.

The most persistent change in the original dialogue is the removal of the word 'God' so that the play Miller is producing becomes not *Godspeed* but *Hail and Farewell*, and expletives such as "God damn it!" and "What the hell!" are toned down to "Jumping butterballs!" and "What the blazes!" Even many of the bits of business that seem specially suited to one of the Marx brothers prove to have been in the original play e.g. Harpo arriving bare to the waist (cf. his arrival in *Animal Crackers*) so that he can put on more clothes for their escape from the hotel, or Chico *à propos* prisons remarking: "It's not so bad. If you behave, they make you a trustee." While there are some special inventions, it is obvious Ryskind could have gone much further than he did unless, for some reason, there was no time available. We really have to judge the film not as a Marx Brothers picture proper but as a farce played in by the Marxes. As such, it can be called a moderately amusing picture. It would be better had the director, William A. Seiter, not adopted such a dull and repetitive style and had the editing been tighter (there are too many pauses where dialogue could have been overlaid from the next shot and the pace quickened). But the basic limitation is the original play which on a close study does not appear to have been particularly outstanding.

It is misleading that the film does go part of the way towards being a regular Marx picture by keeping the three of them in traditional costume and Harpo mute once more. Certainly there are lines and actions that seem well in character. Helped by such moments, it is possible to visualise how, in a considerably less narrow adaptation, *Room Service* could have approached the usual Marx comedy. And since routine comedies are common enough and Marx Brothers pictures are not, there is the temptation to squeeze as much out of it as possible of the usual Groucho, Harpo and Chico.

*　　*　　*

The central part of the producer Gordon Miller goes straight to Groucho. Miller is fast-talking and resourceful in all the tight corners that keep coming up, as well as being dishonest and unscrupulous. But his dialogue lacks the thrust and sparkle of a genuine Groucho character. In general, Miller is too rational in his methods, too concerned: the old Groucho would face up to each complication as it came instead of trying so hard to avoid it. The old Groucho enjoyed a showdown but Gordon Miller constantly fears one. The hotel manager is Groucho's brother-in-law in the film and it is worrying to contemplate Groucho's having a sister. Also, he is unnaturally silent at times, as when he and Chico are pulling on clothes to leave the hotel. He browbeats the waiter Sasha into bringing them and the play's author some food. "I don't care about food for myself, Sash," he tells the man, "But if you let a great American author starve to death his blood will be on your hands. Do you know what the penalty is for murder in this country?" But his manner of delivery lacks the old ferocity and bite, and again when Groucho tries to obtain food by telephoning down and speaking with a dialect, it is very half-hearted – he starts with the Colonel Hawkins voice from *A Day at the Races* but it quickly slips and fools no-one.

Yet there are a few flashes of the old Groucho. Trying to get rid of the bothersome playwright, he pictures the man's mother sitting by the fireside all alone without him. "We have no fireside," objects the playwright. "Then how do you listen to the President's speeches?" retorts Groucho with a line not found in the play. Later he threatens to see that the obstructive figure of the hotel chief is reduced to a bellboy. "No, that's too good for him. I'll make him a guest." This could be Mr. Hammer speaking in *The Cocoanuts*, or Ronald Kornblow, Groucho's other hotel manager in *A Night in Casablanca*. He slips in a splendid loping walk across the hotel fover, and there is a wonderful glimpse of his furtively cheating himself at patience or solitaire. A nice moment occurs when he introduces Harpo, his general assistant, as "the brains of the organisation". Harpo is standing there, mouth agape, looking as stupid as possible, and Groucho adds tartly: "That'll give you some idea of the organisation."

*　　*　　*

Chico is the director of the play, Harry Binelli (originally Harry Binion). He is quite well suited to the part, and again there are little additions that recall Chico's customary character (though no-

123

thing so great as letting him near a piano). "The rehearsal, she's-a wonderful," reports Chico, "Yes, sirree, it's-a wonderful. I still think it's a terrible play but it makes a wonderful rehearsal." (We never actually see Chico doing any direction but there is every sign that the play is as bad as he maintains.) When Groucho is trying to keep the author happy for fear of losing the play, he doesn't take kindly to all of Chico's remarks and gives him some sour looks. "If you don't mind I'd like to wash up," says the newly arrived young man, unaware of the desperate situation, prompting Chico to remark: "The rest of us are washed up already." Miller in the stage play calls Binion "Harry" but Groucho calls Chico "Binelli" signifying the less cordial relationship that always exists between Groucho and Chico. The "washed up" line is typical of Chico's frankness (in *The Cocoanuts*, it is the first thing we learn about him as he ominously informs Groucho that his empty suitcase will be full up when he leaves). Here again Chico exhibits his one-track mind. Groucho gets the idea that the waiter Sasha could supply them with food. Chico clearly has the same idea so Groucho asks "What do you think, Binelli?" Chico looks the waiter over and considers it, then replies: "He looks just right to me. I could eat him raw." Groucho's idea is the more devious one of giving Sasha a part in the play as a bribe for the food. Similarly, when they have found a backer who protests that he has a weak heart as they press him to sign the contract, Chico's only thought is: "Then sign quickly!"

ROOM SERVICE: The author (Frank Albertson) tries to escape but Groucho and Chico know how to handle him.

Harpo assumes the part of a third character, Faker Englund, who was not as important as Miller or Binion. Most of Faker's lines are given to Chico, either directly or by Chico explaining Faker's actions when in the play he spoke for himself (this interpretative function of Chico's is, of course, a regular feature in the Marx films). Harpo is left with little to do (including no harp) and must have been reminded of that time long before when Uncle Al Shean wrote *Home Again* and put in nothing for him to perform. (But then he is said to have devised most of his material for the stage show of *The Cocoanuts*, and probably a lot in the other films.) At any rate, there are some felicitous moments when he does intervene in the action and he never needed much of a situation to work from for his talent to shine. Harpo's mania for food leads to the engaging spectacle of his stuffing away the dinner brought by Sasha like an automaton. He conveys it to his mouth with no apparent pause for swallowing and chewing, and he doesn't stop when Chico's arm gets caught up with his. He doesn't waste a thing: when Chico throws salt over his shoulder, Harpo's hand is there to snatch at it and he licks it up. Earlier, when a turkey he has brought with him escapes, there is the glorious sight of Harpo's pursuing it around a bedroom with a cudgel, contriving to smash all the most vulnerable objects in range, such as vases and the head of the play's prospective backer.

From Harpo comes another coy confession about his love life but, instead of producing the photograph of a horse (*Animal Crackers*), he brings out a miniature doll. This is useful when he plays sick and the hotel doctor wants him to say "Ah" as he is able to reply by a high-tooting squeak from the toy under the bedclothes. There is an endearingly childish literalness about Harpo when, hearing the ingenuous playwright declare that he has burned his bridges behind him, Harpo lifts up the back of the man's coat and inspects his breeches. Equally childish is the way he keeps drinking the glasses of medicine the hotel chief pours out for the playwright when he has to feign a suicide attempt to delay the closing of his play in the hotel's theatre. Flashes of the true Harpo come when he and Groucho doff their hats, bow, and straighten up with the wrong one, Harpo having deftly switched them over as in *Duck Soup* or *Go West;* while Harpo's chewing a sandwich with the cellophane wrapper still on reminds us of his bizarre sandwiches in *A Night at the Opera* or his snacks during *The Cocoanuts.*

* * *

As a whole, the film (and play) shows a refreshingly scant regard for insanity and death. Neither Groucho nor Chico have any scruples about hocking their author's typewriter, and when the collector (finely played as a slow-witted, timid individual by Philip Loeb) comes for some back payments, they tell him its owner is in an insane

ROOM SERVICE: Groucho and Chico bluff it out with the
ever-gullible hotel chief (Donald MacBride).

asylum. Unfortunately he took the machine with him. As Chico puts
it: "He likes to hear the little bell ring." The hotel doctor is labelled
a quack by Chico, who poses briefly as a rival doctor, and is tied up
in the bathroom. Even in farce, it is quite unbelievable that he should
later emerge and come out on their side against his superior, the
hotel chief. A mock suicide is staged and the hotel chief who cal-
lously plans to close down the play in mid-performance is made to
regret his actions as he looks on the playwright's body and Groucho
and Chico sing "One last sweet cheerio" while Harpo brings in a
wreath to lay on the 'corpse'. It would be quite a touching moment
were it not a ruse.

But at an earlier point when everything seems hopeless, Groucho
looks at Harpo, Chico and the playwright, saying: "Well, the quartet is complete. What shall we do? Sing 'Sweet Adeline'?" Instantly,
one's mind hearkens back to the four stowaways of *Monkey Business*
doing precisely that. Sadly, this is worlds apart.

The gap might have been narrower. Zeppo could have played the
author and given the other three's scenes with the character that
extra stimulation that comes from seeing the four in action. We could,
with some reshaping, have had the pleasure of seeing Siegfried
Rumann, such a fine foil in the two preceding films, as the irate
hotel chief. Instead the role is played on a tiresome level of continual
bluster. Margaret Dumont could have come in as a gullible and long-

suffering potential backer. Certainly Groucho suffers from having no women to insult. (There are two of them around — one of them, Lucille Ball, later to become a noted comedienne — but Groucho gives them no interference.) As it is, we must largely concur with Richard Rowland's remarks [18]: "No ordinary farce hotel room can hold the Marx Brothers; infinity can scarcely hold them. The well-made play — and *Room Service* was such — with its many doors, all carefully planned to supply comic entrances and exits, is too restrictive. The Brothers need Casablanca, where various worlds meet, or the backstage of a theatre, which is whole worlds in itself, or the limitless background of a battlefield or the whole Atlantic Ocean, for their comedy, opening as it does on vast vistas of eternity."

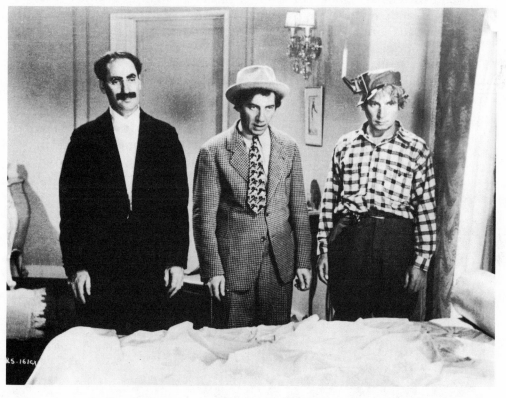

ROOM SERVICE: Groucho, Chico, and Harpo in a moment of reverent silence for the "dead" playwright.

11. At the Circus (1939)

Placing the Marxes against a circus background is a promising idea; but also a demanding one. In previous films the Marxes had rarely fitted in with their settings, being unsympathetic to their values. The circus is a different matter, at least for Chico and Harpo. For as William Whitebait observed in a contemporary review of *At the Circus,* "The circus ring is where by tradition the Marx Brothers belong, with the Fratellinis and the world's best clowns, and to see them swinging on a trapeze, running with the clowns, and firing Margaret Dumont from a cannon, reminds us of the real origins of their humour, which is by no means specifically modern as the surrealist interpreters of it would like to suggest." [21] Unfortunately, there is no real sawdust atmosphere; it seems to have been beyond the writer (Irving Brecher) and director (Edward Buzzell) who have not developed the background or subsidiary characters with any real thought or effort. The opera house, the ocean liner, the sanitarium and the race track were all much more effectively sketched in. This was pretty highly budgeted (at least for certain

AT THE CIRCUS: Even the seal has a badge — only Groucho cannot get on the train.

scenes like the climax at Dukesbury Manor). It is rather a fault of approach that Harpo and Chico do not spring more naturally from this environment. One difficulty is the number of crooks that are operating in it — particularly fellow performers who ought to be incorruptible if the community spirit of circus life means anything. (Groucho obviously moves in more sophisticated surroundings and is properly brought into the world of the circus from outside.)

* * *

The script introduces a young circus operator, Jeff Wilson, about to meet the deadline on a final payment to avoid losing the circus. Chico is Jeff's devoted friend, as he was Judy's in *A Day at the Races*. "I ain't got nothing but you can always have half," Chico tells Jeff and, when he scents trouble, consults his notebook to see who can help out. Just as Chico conjured up Groucho to keep Mrs. Upjohn from leaving the Standish Sanitarium, so here he also summons Groucho into the film by a telegram, this time as a lawyer, J. Cheever Loophole. But it is a point of weakness here that Groucho doesn't come knowing that Margaret Dumont is waiting to be plucked. What attracts him is merely the prospect of earning money. He seems to leave nothing of a practice behind him, carrying his shingle along so that his office is wherever he is. This gives Groucho the right unsettled air but it does somewhat reduce him to be seen not making his own way more successfully.

Chico is also Harpo's friend and serves to introduce him to Groucho, who promptly mistakes him for Jeff Wilson; for, given one look at Harpo's most hideous blank expression, Groucho's immediate assessment is, "He's the executive type." (Cf. *Room Service*, "the brains of the organisation".)

When Jeff is robbed of the vital takings, we again have a more mundane basis for a film than the clash of personalities in *A Night at the Opera*. Groucho, calling himself "the legal eagle", steps in to investigate the robbery. "Watch the eagle swoop down!" he cries, but at the first sight of the suspect, Goliath the Strongman, he quickly backs away. He does here (as at times in other films, especially *Duck Soup*) look like a bird of prey, his black frock coat like the sleek back and folded wings of a bird, his legs bent up almost out of sight, but this impressive appearance is very easily deflated here. Not only does Goliath alarm him (to make up for it, he is unpleasantly aggressive grilling a midget), but he is also taken aback by the sharp sound of a train whistle and a flower (the prop of a magician) that opens unexpectedly as he hands it to the heroine while he is (with rather sickening abasement) promising his help in any way.

At a later stage, Groucho visits another performer, Peerless Pauline, who walks upside down wearing suction boots. He notices her slipping the missing money into her bosom. "There must be some way of getting that money without getting into trouble with the Hays Office," he remarks in an aside. A quick cut to a close-up on Groucho would have let this seem more of a spontaneous ad-lib but instead the camera tracks ponderously in to hear him say it. He suggests she take a walk on the ceiling to dislodge the money but

129

AT THE CIRCUS:
On the train, Harpo
makes Chico realise
what a strong man
he is.

he has to do it as well before she will agree. Groucho puts on a
rather ridiculous costume, and then gets stuck when the money drops
while she swings down to reclaim it. To see him so easily outwitted
marks quite a decline, though it is nothing compared to the parallel
sequence in *Go West*. He may possibly become sympathetic but the
heroic dash of the old Groucho was more valuable. And what do we
say about that further iconoclastic touch whereby he threatens her
with the law? This might just be taken as his threatening her with
his legal skill, but it seems to be rather the customary threat of
calling the police as though Groucho were a solid citizen who relies
on proper procedures instead of being, as previously, a law unto
himself. In this new role, the least he could do would be to solve
the crime, but the money finally reappears by chance (at least he
does a splendid job handling the film's rich Mrs. Dukesbury).

*   *   *

Here Chico becomes an increasingly stupid character, obtuse
without the layer of guile that used to accompany it. He guards the
circus train with the precious money aboard (an index of how much
he is trusted by Jeff). When Groucho arrives in the pouring rain,
he can't get on without a pass badge, despite the fact that Chico
has summoned him. Harpo comes along with hundreds of the right
badges inside his coat (he is always more than able to meet such a
challenge); even the seal he is escorting under an umbrella (demonstrating his kindness to animals) proves to have a badge. Groucho
has to settle for a few sly remarks about Chico's state of develop-
ment. "I haven't seen you since I stopped taking Scott's Emulsion,"
he remarks in response to Chico's infantile manner, and when he
mentions a Hot Toddy he adds, "It's a drink" for Chico's benefit.
Eventually Chico relents and gives him a badge, but he still can't
get on because it turns out to be last year's badge, and he is rudely

pushed back into a puddle. The inspiration for this scene is obviously the one at the speakeasy door in *Horse Feathers* but that was brilliant and this is stupid. It is not so well written and, whereas Chico didn't know Groucho in *Horse Feathers* and so had no reason to let him in, here he has himself summoned Groucho and it seems excessively nonsensical of him to obstruct an ally like this. Similarly Chico blocks Groucho's every attempt to obtain a cigar from the midget to compare with the butt found at the scene of the crime. Each time he asks for one of the midget's cigars, Chico asininely offers him one of his own. When Chico sabotages Groucho's auction in *The Cocoanuts* with the same unyielding persistence, it is funny because Groucho himself arranged for Chico to do it. The humour lies not in Chico's stupidity but in the way Groucho's underhand scheming rebounds on him. The cigar scene is stupid without point, for both are concerned to solve the crime.

* * *

Harpo is on the whole better served. Again he works for one of the bad guys, Goliath, as his assistant and is roughly treated, for an innocent mistake during a performance of Goliath's act. He gets on well with animals, playing draughts with the seal and pacifying the lions with his trumpet, both showing a power of communion with dumb animals (the dumb speaking to the dumb). This gift is equated by some susceptible negro circus hands with mesmerism and Harpo is likened to Svengali. This leads into another song and dance session followed by his harping, but one that is less elaborate and **artistic than that of** *A Day at the Races*.

There is also a chance for Harpo to hit Chico when Chico decides to "re-destruct" the crime and gives Harpo the role of the crook. Harpo resents this as a slur on his character, though he later produces evidence of a criminal past, a wanted notice reading "Fifty cents reward for jaywalking" (cf. *The Cocoanuts*). To Chico this proves that crime doesn't pay: you don't get enough for jaywalking. Chico explains to Harpo that he merely has to act the crook: Harpo's childish notion of acting leads him to kiss his way up Chico's arm, getting so carried away that he almost has Chico on the floor a moment later. As they re-enact the crime, Harpo enthusiastically whacks Chico over the head. Chico decides for safety's sake to reverse their roles but the moment he announces he is the crook Harpo takes him at his word and whacks him again. (Harpo does everything wholeheartedly, like the spectacular sneeze that wrecks the midget's house.) Perhaps the finest example of Harpo's physical humour occurs in his rescue of Groucho from his predicament in Peerless Pauline's tent, hanging upside down. Harpo speedily solves the problem by undoing Groucho's boots, letting him fall to the floor even more painfully than when he missed Harpo's net in *Horse Feathers*. The quickest way is the quickest way — as when Harpo sticks dynamite into the vase on Groucho's head in *Duck Soup* —

and Harpo shows as little respect for any practical limitations as Chico does in his thinking, e.g. "You pay him enough he could sail yesterday" in *A Night at the Opera*.

One of the best scenes concerns Chico and Harpo's search of Goliath's apartment while the strongman is asleep in the lower bunk. Chico reckons that if he becomes restless, they will soothe him back to sleep like a baby. Harpo helpfully produces a baby's bottle full of milk. Chico decides they will work in the dark. Harpo puts on dark glasses. They start and make a noise at which Goliath stirs. Chico snaps out the light and Goliath puts it on. Harpo, occupying a coat hanging from a hook (as in *Horse Feathers*), turns it out. When everything is quiet, Harpo switches the light on again, falls out of the coat and goes across to join Chico who is hiding in the upper bunk. Chico starts down and crunches Harpo's hand. Harpo grasps it in agony and rushes to the cabinet over the washbasin, pours a dark liquid on it and rubs his hand up and down on the door like a paintbrush (his hands take on this limp, lifeless quality in *A Night at the Opera* when crushed in a piano lid).

They start to search Goliath himself who has, unco-operatively, gone to sleep grasping the top of the blanket with his hands while the lower end is wrapped tightly around his feet. Harpo scissors across the blanket just short of his hands and feet, and looks around.

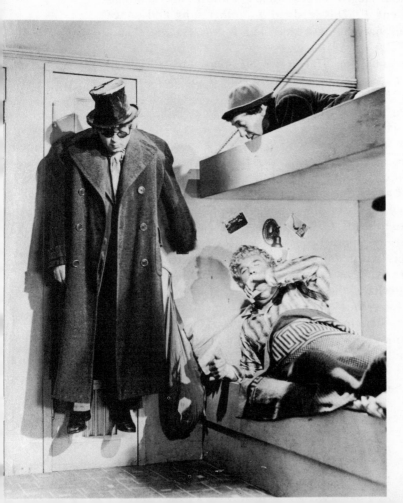

AT THE CIRCUS:
As Goliath (Nat Pendleton) stirs, Harpo, hiding on a clothes hook, turns out the light while Chico watches from the upper bunk.

Chico pulls out a pillow and opens it, letting fluff drift all over the room. Harpo picks up a pad of cotton wool, clenches it between his teeth, pads his stomach, rings a bell and waves a spittoon like a Santa Claus collecting for charity amidst the swirling snow of fluff. It is an instant, magical, and hilarious transformation, all the funnier because this distraction has occurred at such an unsuitable time and place. Chico helps it along by singing 'Jingle Bells' and dropping a coin in the spittoon. Like the burglary in *Duck Soup* or the switching of paintings in *Animal Crackers*, it shows that Harpo and Chico aren't suited to quiet underhand operations. Goliath is shifting uneasily so Chico concocts a sleeping draught. Harpo promptly swallows it (like the medicine in *Room Service*) and passes out. Chico tries slapping his face and telling him to wake up, alternating this with snatches of a lullaby to soothe the restless giant.

Harpo comes round and slits open Goliath's mattress, clambering inside to search it. Goliath sits up as Harpo tunnels underneath him. A horn sounds, as it does beneath the Lemonade Seller in *Duck Soup*. Goliath decides he would be better off in the top bunk and swings his mattress up there on top of Chico. He settles down on top of both of them — another human sandwich like that of *Monkey Business*. When Chico and Harpo get free, Chico slaps Harpo vigorously as a long stream of compressed fluff issues from his mouth.

* * *

Groucho's songs are always a treat and he performs here one about Lydia, the tattooed lady, whose body was an education in it-

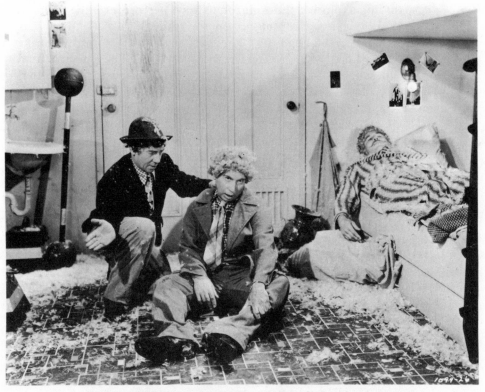

AT THE CIRCUS: During their search of Goliath's apartment, Harpo swallows the sleeping draught prepared for the restless giant and Chico tries to slap him out of his torpor.

AT THE CIRCUS: Groucho tightens the "nuts" on the back of the dress of Mrs. Dukesbury (Margaret Dumont).

self and on one part of which could be found none other than Captain Spaulding exploring the Amazon. (Chico performs on the piano in the same setting, a restaurant car on the train.)

But perhaps the highlight of Groucho's appearance comes when he storms Dukesbury Manor after learning that Jeff has a rich aunt who could save the circus. He races around Whitcomb, the butler, who feebly blocks his way, telling him that he's Mr. Dukesbury. The camera travels with Groucho, reinforcing this charge through the portals of snobbery. After likening the place to a hotel (cf. *Animal Crackers*), he ascends the stairs and bellows down the corridors: "Oh, larooo! Mrs. Dukesbury! Yahooo!" "What in the world . . ." remarks Margaret Dumont as Groucho sweeps into her boudoir. "Keep your shirt on," he tells her, "I'm looking for old lady Dukesbury." She identifies herself. "Snookums!" he cries, rushing to her side and clasping her hand as he kneels. She doesn't know him. "You mean you've forgotten. I know, you have forgotten! Those June nights on the Riviera when we sat beneath those shimmering skies moonlight bathing in the Mediterranean. We were young, gay, reckless! That night I drank champagne from your slipper. Two quarts. It would have held more but you were wearing inner soles." Again his lyrical outpourings come down to earth — with another reflection on her size (here of her feet, cf. being like an office block in *Duck Soup*). Margaret Dumont and Whitcomb have been the first two people over whom he has been able to assert himself but sadly, after this promising beginning, the scene degenerates quickly. Groucho's dialogue, as when explaining fluctuation in a French accent, is feeble and forced. At least he soon has a nice moment, reflecting a new found thrift (the reverse of his former wastefulness) as he pockets all her cigars. From this scene emerges the fact that a big *soirée* is being held and the select four hundred of Newport are being invited to hear Jardinet and his entire symphony orchestra who are coming all the way from Paris. Groucho tries to stop Jardinet ever landing but his 'FBI message' to the boat is not very inspired — the moment he mentions a dope ring, we half-know he will have to call Jardinet the "head dope".

* * *

This brings about the climax in which Harpo and Chico show Jardinet and his musicians to their specially built floating orchestral platform, get them started, cut the mooring ropes, and let them drift out to sea playing the Prelude to Act 3 of Wagner's 'Lohengrin' to an audience of seagulls. Jeff Wilson sets up his circus on the front lawn of Dukesbury Manor while Groucho is inside at the dinner keeping an eye on things. This is an operation on a scale that recalls the opera being wrecked or the race meeting delayed. Groucho counts heads as the four hundred arrive (it emphasises them as a mere

AT THE CIRCUS: Groucho tells Margaret Dumont just how feverishly he loves her while a giraffe licks her back and gives her the greatest sensual thrill of her entire film relationship with Groucho.

number, not individual people), makes another introduction for Margaret Dumont (she will be saying "a few boring words") and holds the guests there until Jeff is ready. Groucho wields the weight of decorum to his advantage by taking further cups of coffee after the other guests have all finished, which is more than enough to keep the four hundred waiting, making them not only nameless but sheeplike in obeying the laws of etiquette. He also passes the time declaring to la Dumont how feverishly he loves her just as a giraffe puts its head through the window and licks her exposed shoulder, giving her the greatest sensual thrill of her entire relationship with Groucho.

Behind all this lies the assumption that the guests, although they have assembled to hear highbrow music, would much rather taste the simple, undemanding pleasures of the circus. It is just that it is not socially dignified to do so. But here, given the opportunity, they are quite happy to be ushered into their seats without any protest as Jardinet drifts forgotten along Atlantic shipping lanes. Margaret Dumont herself relaxes sufficiently in the end to share a Coke with Groucho, each with different straws in the happiest-ever image of the two of them together. However, there is a more spectacular entertainment laid on than anyone planned and Margaret Dumont being despatched by cannon to cling as part of a human chain swinging above ground is quite something, if (of necessity) marred by the special effects it entails. On the ground, Groucho rises to the occasion with another commentary. Soon the money appears, saving Jeff, and Mrs. Dukesbury, back on terra firma, is delighted with the success of her evening. In fact, everyone has enjoyed letting their hair down and this is perhaps the key lesson of the Marx initiative — the fun of shedding inhibitions.

12. Go West (1940)

Go West starts rather promisingly. Although deprived of his standard costume and dressed in a rather too fanciful outfit, Groucho makes an imposing entry, striding into a station booking hall followed by a long line of porters. They come to a halt. "Any of you boys got change of ten cents?" he asks. They haven't. "Well ... keep the baggage!" The booking clerk then spots that he is ten dollars short for a ticket to the West. Chico and Harpo approach. It turns out that Harpo is heading west, too, but he has only ten dollars. Explaining what he did with the rest, he outlines a wavy shape, the one that Chico mistook for a snake in *A Day at the Races,* and grins wickedly. Chico guesses a snake again but realises he has spent it on a woman a moment later. So the position is that Harpo has exactly the sum left that Groucho needs to buy a ticket. Conversely, Groucho has just the right amount to enable Harpo to do the same. This is the set-up for a scene in which Groucho (far from his natural habitat in the rich widow belt) is reduced to fleecing Chico and Harpo; but they outsmart him at every turn. In part it recalls Groucho acting the sucker for Chico in *A Day at the Races* at the racetrack, while its technique is the one used in trying to pay the sheriff his feedbill in that same film, except here the banknote is on a thread.

Chico explains that his brother Harpo is going west to pick the gold right off the street. Harpo produces a shovel and practises scooping it up. Groucho, confident he faces a pair of absolute simpletons, moves into action, warning them that out west they shoot at anything that looks eastern. "Why, they'd blow his head off if he was out west with that flea incubator. How much did it cost him?"

GO WEST: A posed shot that sums up the opening scene in the railway station.

A Western style hat will cost ten dollars. Chico counters by offering one. "Well, I'll take it," says Groucho, adding truthfully, "But I'm only making a buck on it." Harpo hauls out his piggy bank which is hidden in his pants on the far end of a length of string. He hands over a note which Groucho quickly pockets. Chico has to remind him that it's a ten spot which requires nine dollars change. As Groucho reluctantly counts out the nine, Harpo retrieves the ten spot by pulling on the thread which is attached to it. And so it goes on, Harpo gaining a complete Western outfit and Groucho losing his savings.

What makes this scene so richly amusing is that Groucho, who considers himself a slicker quite capable of handling a pair of fools like these and practising the most obvious tricks, is so thoroughly and deservedly hoodwinked himself. Groucho never was a match for either brother. Here, more than just defeating Groucho, they benefit themselves (as Chico did with his racing tip, but previously he didn't gain from these encounters — he just frustrated Groucho).

* * *

It is all the more worth recalling this scene in detail as it is the only good one in *Go West*. For, once the Marx Brothers actually move out to the West, they prove to be no match at all for the inhabitants until the climax. One doesn't expect to find Chico confiding nervously to Harpo, "Rusty, I no like-a the West", the moment they get out there. Groucho goes out with no kind of status and there is no Margaret Dumont or Siegfried Rumann for him to take a firm hand with.

All three Marxes become a laughing stock in the Crystal Palace Saloon in the town. Playing S. Quentin Quale (a vulgar insider's joke as "San Quentin quail" was slang for promiscuous, under-age girls who could get a man a stiff jail sentence) he restyles himself "Two Gun Quale" and has trouble keeping his gun belt up; but after creating a tense moment or two his entrance gives way to anti-climax. Harpo and Chico hand over an I.O.U. for drinks to the bartender which is considered hilariously funny. Harpo prepares to draw

GO WEST: Chico and Harpo have an idea in the baggage car of the train during the climax.

on Red Baxter, the town boss, but his gun becomes a clothes brush, though redeemingly the brush then turns out to be a gun that goes

GO WEST: Watched by Chico and Groucho, Harpo explains how he expects to go West and scoop the gold right off the streets.

off unexpectedly. But after this the pair get bounced out.

In other familiar ways, the Marxes are diminished. Chico and Harpo are kind and considerate, ready to loan an old prospector enough money for a grubstake. When they have lost the man's security, which transpires to be a valuable land deed, they go with Groucho to commiserate with the man's daughter who becomes the film's heroine.

All the material is so much worse. It is a great shame that Bert Kalmar and Harry Ruby, originally announced to write the picture, did not in fact do so. There are many feeble jokes and weak scenes. In a crowded stage coach (not comparable to the crowded cabin of *A Night at the Opera*, because it doesn't build in the same way, nor does it have the pith of Margaret Dumont being expected), a mother has only to say that her baby can't stand "the jerks in the coach" for Harpo and Chico to rise and make for the door.

And what does one say in mitigation for such scenes as that in which Groucho sets out to make a tough deal with Red Baxter in exchange for the land deed, has it taken away from him, and gets nothing in return? He tries threatening the law (an unmistakable weakness here, whatever might be argued when this occurs in *At the Circus*), and Baxter indulges in some fancy shooting to warn him off it. When Groucho picks out an exact target as though he were about to reply with some even fancier shooting, hopes are raised. Baxter peers hard and can just about discern the target. "What good eyesight you've got!" comments Groucho and lets it go at that. This comic let-down would best suit the Bob Hope type of picture but it is not the old Groucho who could always assert himself so effortlessly. Here, as he leaves, he is tripped and falls down some stairs in full view of the town. Chico and Harpo revive him to hear him say, "I was going to thrash them within an inch of their lives but I didn't have a tape-measure." This is merely a variation on "I'd horsewhip you if I had a horse" in *Horse Feathers* where Groucho idly used it to browbeat Zeppo and was in full command; here he has a real reason for thrashing someone but is sadly incapable of dealing with him either verbally or physically. He was kicked

GO WEST: Harpo prepares to shoot it out with the town boss, Red Baxter (Robert Barrat), but he turns out to have holstered a clothes brush.

down a longer flight of stairs in *A Night at the Opera* but there he concocted a magnificent revenge. Here his next attempt to recover the situation goes wrong as well.

Late at night, he, Chico, and Harpo, creep back to Baxter's office to steal the deed. They make enough noise to be detected and a couple of the saloon's floosies come in to keep Groucho and Chico occupied while Red Baxter is called. The girls bring in some bottles and, although Groucho and Chico are confident they can get the girls drunk, things unfortunately happen the other way around. (Earlier one of these girls was delegated by Red Baxter to entertain Groucho and towed him away with the words "Come on, son." Groucho meekly accepted their dominance by saying to Red, "Goodbye, daddy.")

At least, Harpo, busily blowing the safe in the next room, maintains his dignity here and has the respect of the girls: "That redhead, he's a demon!" one of them remarks. He is clever enough to let one of the floosies pour her drink away into his top hat and he also removes a tiara from them with a magnet. He gains a lot of fun opening the safe, for instance with a stick of dynamite that turns out to be a Christmas cracker (like the gun becoming a brush) which then explodes (like the brush going off). Another slight redeeming factor of this scene is Groucho's way of stretching out on a couch with one of the girls, in which he has one leg stuck naturally halfway up into the air, the kind of reclining position that goes quite logically with somebody of his strange upright shape. The scene also ends amiably in a pastiche of the traditional western in which the villains and the good guys keep arriving alternately and holding the others up.

The climax, too, with the Marx Brothers racing the villains and battling with them on a train, is quite amusing. But the trouble is that it would be just about as amusing if it featured Abbott and Costello or Martin and Lewis. Its jokes are largely mechanical and achieved with a lot of trick work and special effects. At one point Harpo lies straddled between two carriages holding the train together. He slowly stretches as the gap is widened and a good idea is marred in the execution (perhaps inevitably outside the cartoon field) as it is too obvious where Harpo's legs really end and the extension begins (and the stretching should be all over). Earlier tricks with Harpo's anatomy like the leg-pulling and hand-wringing of *Monkey Business* were much more convincing. *Go West* has the same kind of fault in the last shot as Harpo knocks a railroad president into the ground — like the moment in *At the Circus* when Harpo sinks under the weight of a dumb-bell, it is spoilt by the way a prepared hole is seen to open up.

"**Brake! The brake!**" yells Groucho as the train hurtles on, and Harpo obligingly breaks the brake and throws it away. This is a line

Harpo can get away with better than most comedians, but it is very contrived compared to "Tie on-a the bed, throw the rope out of the window" in *Horse Feathers* where we delightedly know what will happen on Chico's insistence while here we have to figure out the joke and it rates something of a groan.

There is an objection, also, to the way the train in this climactic scene runs off the track and pushes a house along in front of it, as the owner has done nothing to deserve having his home wrecked. Theoretically, too, the railroad should in some way deserve having its track and train so heavily damaged as Morgan's race track and Gottlieb's opera company asked to be sabotaged.

* * *

The curiously good opening scene apart, it is hard to imagine writers being so unsympathetic to what the Marx Brothers had built up in the past: basically a world in which *they* order events. There is nothing wrong with the switch to a period setting, and the team have survived without Margaret Dumont before (*Monkey Business, Horse Feathers;* and this film does have the beginnings of a substitute Thelma Todd figure in June MacCloy's Lulubelle). It is puzzling how Irving Brecher, who achieved some moderately pleasing results with *At the Circus,* could have lapsed into this, though a credit for 'Original Screenplay' implies that other hands came in later. Whoever they were, they failed to include anyone who understood the Marx Brothers. Most of *Go West* is an insipid pot-pourri of misunderstanding.

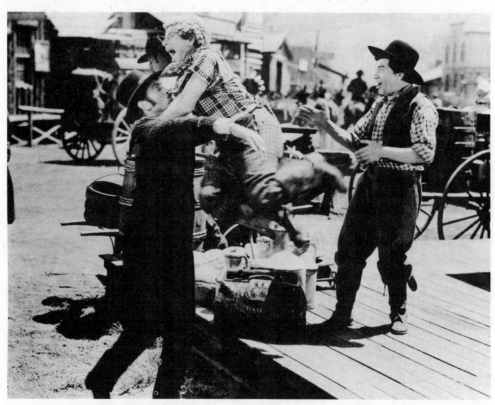

GO WEST: Harpo and Chico enthusiastically greet Beecher (Walter Woolf King).

13. The Big Store (1941)

The Marxes had made tentative announcements about retiring from the screen before. They were discontented with their recent work, and not without cause. It appears that *The Big Store* was meant to be a signing-off: Harpo was to retire, Chico to set up a band, Groucho to go into radio.

At any rate, *The Big Store* marks a recovery from the depths touched by parts of *Go West*. Like *Go West*, it is a film with only one outstanding long scene (Groucho and Harpo encountering Margaret Dumont), but there are some other good touches and even when it is flat and uninspired it generally has the right approach. This is not surprising as its story is by Nat Perrin who with Arthur Sheekman wrote additional dialogue for *Duck Soup* and a radio series for Groucho and Chico called *Flywheel and Shyster* (Groucho is a Wolf J. Flywheel in this film). It is just not well enough written to compare with the first two M-G-M films but it seems part of the same world. We go through familiar types of situation and there is some impression of fresh thinking.

The characters of Groucho, Chico and Harpo have been changed. However precariously, they have become more settled as though accepting the mantle of middle age. Groucho has given up chasing rich widows and entered on a credible and seedy decline as an unsuccessful private eye, Wolf J. Flywheel — 'BLOODHOUNDS TRANSFUSED — FINGER PRINTS MANICURED — GIN RUMMY'. This follows logically from his impoverished air in *At the Circus*. Here he doesn't even winkle out Margaret Dumont: instead, in an unprecedented reversal, she comes to him, and the new desperation of Groucho is evident in the efforts he makes to snare not just her but any customer who should happen to appear. The old indifference and incompetence asserts itself in time but he works hard getting his big chance, mindful possibly of the poem he recites in a later solo appearance in *Double Dynamite*, 'Gather Ye Rosebuds.'

As for Harpo, he takes on the innovatory role of assistant to Groucho as well as preserving the customary tie to Chico (here, as in *Go West*, being Chico's brother). This makes the firmest connection between the three since *Monkey Business* (excluding the special case of *Room Service*). Groucho and Chico don't seem to have met officially before the film starts but Groucho gets in a typical dig as Chico is photographing him with the instructions, "Look at me and laugh." "I've been doing that for years," replies Groucho, slipping out of character to look back on their past encounters, or indulge in some family ribbing.

Groucho's job is still on the fringe of society, and Harpo can't have many qualifications or feel very secure working for this employer. At any rate Chico seems to have found a solid, respectable job, running a music conservatory. He teaches children to play the piano and when his back is turned they imitate his shooting-the-keys technique with their index finger. With this spreading, one can see Chico's conservatory leaving its trademark on the (probably horrified) music world. The place has a friendly atmosphere and Chico largely abandons the crooked, wily outlook he had before. His most successful graduate, and good friend, is Tommy Rogers who is about to inherit a department store and promises to sell it to build Chico a new and better conservatory.

The plot of *The Big Store* is corny and contrived. It weighs too heavily on the proceedings but at least it has the merit of involving Margaret Dumont from the start (in *At the Circus* she came in very late). She plays Tommy's aunt, Martha Phelps, and the name isn't quite august enough for this grand actress. The villain is Douglas Dumbrille (Morgan in *A Day at the Races*); as Grover, manager of the big store, he has been cooking the books and is trying to rub out Tommy and marry his rich aunt who stands to inherit the store on Tommy's death.

*　*　*

Before Margaret Dumont encounters Groucho, we discover him stretched out on the couch in his office, reading a newspaper and idly following the physical exercises being dictated by the radio. When they presume to command him to stand on his head, he flicks the switch over to some light music and gets up to eat his breakfast which is laid out on his desk by Harpo, wearing an eyeshade across his forehead as a symbol of his position. "Take this paper out and sell it!" orders Groucho, exhibiting a meanness worthy of Jack Benny and a concern over pennies that shows a new financial caution on Groucho's part. Harpo is on his way out when he spots Martha Phelps arriving. Groucho's efforts to make a good impression on her give him a quite new appearance. Food and drink, including a steaming pot of coffee, go into the desk drawers; the bed goes upright into the wall; the 'phones ring as Groucho presses a button at his feet. Mrs. Phelps stands on the welcome rug by the door, distinctly impressed by the hive of activity she has uncovered. Eventually Groucho finds a moment between calls to let her start explaining that her nephew's life is in danger. Harpo dutifully takes a record on the typewriter; but it operates at the decibel level of a road-drill and she can't make herself heard. They struggle on against the clatter of the machine which at one point looks as though it also empties toast when the toaster next to it goes off. It does, however, disgorge its carriage which flies over to land on Groucho's

144

desk. Harpo rushes across, not wasting a second as his super-efficient secretary, but seizes the 'phone instead of the carriage. What is so splendidly absurd about all this is the inverted non-sense of it. Groucho could order Harpo to stop making the noise and Harpo himself cannot possibly hear what is being said to take it down anyway. But the kind of rules the Marxes follow preclude any sensible solution. We half-accept the logic of Groucho and Margaret Dumont struggling on, trying to make each other hear by getting close together at the corner of the desk as Harpo resumes. By now the coffee is boiling over and Groucho tells her, "I'm dripping with offers", as it has spurted over his pinstripes. Harpo further reveals the extent of Groucho's pre-planning by taking in a telegram from a fake hand attached to the back of a door, and industriously dashes across to bring it to Groucho's attention. He turns down its offer in favour of Mrs. Phelps, letting her have his services for a mere $ 6,000 but readily backing down to $ 500 with a $ 5 advance (the old flitting be-

THE GOOKIE: Here is Harpo demonstrating this ghastly expression (from A DAY AT THE RACES). And right, THE BIG STORE: Harpo on roller skates during the big climax.

tween extremes).

The place is now like a steam room and they beat a hasty retreat. As soon as Mrs. Phelps has stepped off the doormat, Groucho picks it up and puts it on (an extreme economy contrasting with his old extravagance again). Harpo dutifully brushes the dust (and most of the hair) off it. Outside Groucho shows her to the company's ramshackle car, a wreck eventually reclaimed by the finance company, a small victory considering its condition and the number of years service it has given (inscribed on the back are the words 'Welcome to Admiral Dewey, Hero of Manila' which dates it back to 1899 at least). Harpo has a fit of giggles at the prospect of driving Mrs. Phelps in it. Wearing his chauffeuring outfit — squashed top hat, gloves, and underwater goggles (suggesting that, when he drives it, it is apt to go strange places) — he gets the vehicle moving. Mrs. Phelps's seat collapses under her — a protection, Groucho quickly declares, against flying bullets. Outside the store, Harpo opens the door only to have it come off completely. Left alone, he starts clearing out the car until he comes under the surveillance of a cop. Just as Chico and the playwright reversed their packing under scrutiny in *Room Service*, so Harpo neatly reverses himself and throws all the junk back in. Later he makes a rare appeal to authority by making the cop shift a car that has parked by a hydrant. When the cop has moved on, Harpo drives his car into the space and throws his lightweight dummy hydrant into the back. This exhibits the same cunning as Harpo's set of portable lamp posts for dog-catching in *Horse Feathers*.

* * *

In the store Groucho is taken by Mrs. Phelps into Grover's office. He immediately spots in Grover someone ripe for insult and the scene provides a brisk display of Groucho's incompetence and rudeness. He strides in and flings his hat towards a wall-lamp, disregarding its failure to lodge there. Grover has merely to ask "How do you do?" for Groucho to take umbrage and declare, "That's rather a personal question, isn't it?" Mrs. Phelps introduces Groucho as a new floorwalker, a job that will let him keep an eye on Tommy. Grover eyes him with a suspicion akin to Whitmore looking at the new doctor in *A Day at the Races*. Again his credentials are questioned. Groucho considers himself highly qualified for the job: "I was a shoplifter for three years" (cf. "Something terribly exciting happened during the 'flu epidemic ... I got the 'flu", when his experience was also on the wrong side). When he incompetently lets slip that he is a detective, Grover finds this even less likely than his being a floorwalker. "If he's a detective," declares Grover, "I'm a monkey's uncle." Groucho's comeback is obvious. It wasn't particularly strong on a previous appearance — when Jennings said "If this is a singing lesson, I'm a ring-tailed monkey" in *Horse*

Feathers. However, Harpo has a very nice moment in this scene when he turns up with Mrs. Phelps's missing purse. Congratulated on his honesty of character, he gets so carried away he even brings out the money that was in it.

When Harpo meets his friend Chico, he gets him to scratch his back (which again likens him to an animal) and they are soon helping to round up a horde of children loose in the bedding department — a tiresome sequence making somewhat questionable humour out of an Italian's large family. The man is also a friend of Chico which suggests misleadingly that Chico is a real Italian, as a phoney ought not to be warmly received.

When Groucho learns that a pair of assassins in raincoats are out to kill Tommy Rogers, he delegates Chico and Harpo to deal with it and calmly goes back to sleep in the bedding department. Chico and Harpo perform a piano duet (the first time they have really played together) during which they also do a form of conga, circling around, over and under each other while keeping up their playing — ostensibly to draw a large crowd so that they can look for the two killers. They find them just in time to save Groucho further embarrassment from having mistakenly captured two men in raincoats who came to discuss buying the store.

Soon after Harpo is told by Chico that his dress is not formal enough for the impending ceremony of handing over the store. He eyes a store mannequin dressed in a dandy's costume. The next mo-

THE BIG STORE: A pensive moment for the villainous Grover (Douglas Dumbrille) as Groucho worms his way into the confidence of Mrs. Phelps (Margaret Dumont) and her nephew Tommy (Tony Martin).

ment the costume is on him, periwig, lace and all. He plays some Mozart on the harp in this period costume and setting (much more appropriate for the instrument than the usual ones) and is backed by two reflections of himself in mirrors. After a while the reflections quite abandon keeping in time with him and even take up different instruments like the violin and bass, confounding Harpo at first; but then, as he realises there is no harm in it, he nods cheerily and carries on his own playing. It is a felicitous sequence and one that stirs up in the gentlest way the identity theme once more. Grouchos proliferated in *Duck Soup* and were all taken by Margaret Dumont as being the genuine article. Here Harpo takes the reflections as himself but they cheekily assume a separate existence. Quite unnecessarily, this is passed off as a dream sequence.

The film's climax, like the hectic trainride of *Go West,* will amuse the undiscerning audience. But the same criticisms apply: the ending would suit any team of comedians whereas the football game, the war, the wrecking of the opera, etcetera, were all stamped with the Marx signature. Here as the Marxes chase and are chased around the big store, swinging on lamps, jumping over rolls of lino, skating along counters and so on, the doubling is too obvious (the stuntman with the Groucho moustache just isn't Groucho) and the film is speeded up to force the laughs.

However, *The Big Store* has its points. Groucho's role is interesting though it has few memorable lines, while Chico suffers from having little to do (he doesn't even manage to interpret one of Harpo's mimed messages). But Harpo emerges strongly and at times becomes the old *enfant terrible.* Its faults are not so severe as those of the two previous M-G-M films and it would have left one reasonably hopeful for the future if it wasn't announced as their farewell picture. It is more fitted for the task than their actual last film, *Love Happy.* But before that they made a comeback with a film that is quite worth having — *A Night in Casablanca.*

THE BIG STORE: Chauffeur Harpo stands by as private eye Groucho gives a helping hand to his wealthy client (Margaret Dumont as Martha Phelps).

14. A Night in Casablanca (1946)

"After Thalberg's death my interest in the movies waned", writes Groucho. "I continued to appear in them, but my heart was in the Highlands. The fun had gone out of picture-making. I was like an old pug, still going through the motions, but now doing it solely for the money. My swan song was *A Night in Casablanca*. This was an independent venture and we were going to get a percentage of the profits." [11] Groucho goes on to write of how time was telling on them — and sadly it was. They may not be as limber as before but this doesn't show. What does — and particularly in Harpo — is their age. After all, Chico was about 55, Harpo 52 and Groucho 50. Harpo's age shows much less in the later *Love Happy* and some of his TV appearances in the fifties. His wig is less extensive here and this tends to throw emphasis on his face. It seems a contradiction for so magical a clown to be unable to resist the inroads of age. Mellowing may sit well on the melancholy clown who can appeal for sympathy but Harpo is still above sentimentality. Yet without the flush of youth, the clown of mischief looks foolish and desperate, a man unable to be his age. Harpo's performance is as sure as ever but tinged by this thought. Age makes no difference really to Chico; and Groucho, if no longer the young wolf, is no less effective as an ageing roué, his strange lope perhaps becoming attributable to arthritis.

On the whole the critics were delighted to see them back, though *The Times'* recognition of this event in its fourth leader led off: "There will be something like mourning among Marxists in London this week." Most of the critics thought it a bad film but didn't care, for, as James Agee put it: "The worst they might ever make would be better worth seeing than most other things I can think of".[1] His further comments get to the heart of the matter: "Many of the things in this one which by substance and look should be level with their best fall somehow flat. The only two reasons I can get wind of are the manufacture of repetition and the fact — they work too well for it to show obviously — that after all these years the Brothers are tired." What a pity that Preston Sturges, the comic genius of the early forties who made a game attempt to revive Harold Lloyd in the production *Mad Wednesday* didn't try to revitalise the Marx Brothers. The main trouble with *A Night in Casablanca* is that what was fresh in a thirties setting (and still is) had become more or less conventional by the forties. There is a feeling of the routine about the film, a lack of ambition, a failure to explore new directions and explode new subjects. As late as the 1960s, Billy Wilder, a director notably ahead of public taste, planned to do just this with the Marx Brothers. "We want to make a satire on the deterioration of diplomatic behaviour, on brinksmanship, wild jokes about the H-bomb — that type of stuff" — in other words, a *Duck Soup* of the sixties, with a United Nations background for the Marx Brothers to run loose in. Unfortunately, for all the details Billy Wilder elaborated [36], this was one project that never came off.

A Night in Casablanca is incapable of dealing with the post-war era. In fact, its inspiration is the escapist cinema's own espionage cycle, particularly *Casablanca*. The similarity extends beyond the title: the police rounding up "the usual suspects" is a close copy of this happening in the Warner film up to the point of a suspicious character being found. Whereas Warners' suspect runs away and is shot down, the cop who rounds up Harpo, idly leaning against a wall, asking him sarcastically if he's holding it up, finds that Harpo is telling the truth when he nods in agreement and the entire building collapses without him. (This sight gag was apparently contributed by Frank Tashlin who was employed by Harpo to devise material for him and who now has quite a reputation in the comedy field — his Martin and Lewis comedy *Artists and Models* is said to contain a parody of a Chico-Harpo mime sequence.) Another quote from a Warner film comes as the vamp Beatrice Rheiner says to Groucho that she will be singing just for him at the cabaret. "You don't have to sing for me — just whistle," replies Groucho in a husky, romantic voice. The reference is to Lauren Bacall's "If you want

A NIGHT IN
CASABLANCA:
Groucho eyes the
artful Chico
with suspicion
while a serious-
faced Harpo watches.

me, just whistle" in *To Have and Have Not.*

Films such as these could have been punishingly parodied but, perhaps through legal difficulties, they are not. *A Night in Casablanca* has a feeble plot of its own to follow, is not so well cast nor so fluently made, lacking the tightly hermetic atmosphere and rich detail of these films. The background is certainly not realistic either but only thin and artificial. To judge from a paperback based on the original screenplay,[2] it seems to have undergone a lot of last minute changes (and some beneficial deletions), suggesting insufficient preparation. At least Siegfried Rumann, now plain Sig Ruman, makes a welcome reappearance as the intemperate Nazi villain.

The wheel turns and here is Groucho once more a hotel manager. Many of his lines as Ronald Kornblow could come from Mr. Hammer in *The Cocoanuts* (but would have been funnier in 1929). The staff are assembled to meet him. "Never mind the staff!" he cries, "Assemble the guests. I'll tell them what I expect of them." He elaborates on this. It means first of all: "Courtesy towards the employees. They must learn that a kind word will get them further with a bellboy or a chambermaid than a couple of drinks. Of course a kind word *and* a couple of drinks will get them still further . . . and if it gets them any further than that, it will get them thrown out of the hotel." These lines have the right feel to them if ending up with a surprisingly moral outlook for Groucho to take, though his further idea shows that the old sense of mischief isn't dead: "The next thing I'm going to do is to change all the numbers on all the rooms." "But the guests!" splutters one of his employers, "They will go into the wrong rooms. Think of the confusion!" "Yeah," retorts Groucho, "But think of the fun!" Time has passed and no longer can Groucho's eccentricities be accepted with just a bewildered shrug. Here he is regarded as an incompetent fool by his superiors and only keeps his job because, unknown to him, all the previous managers have met sudden deaths and no one else will take it. Even so, there is a limit and he is jailed on suspicion of fixing the gambling tables. This situation marks a further stage in the reduction of Groucho. In the early films he was fully accepted for what he was; with the M-G-M period he starts to be questioned, and in *A Day at the Races* he is not merely incompetent but practises a deception posing as a real doctor. Here it is exactly the reverse of that film and it is Groucho who is being duped. It diminishes him considerably not to have the upper hand but to become an innocent stooge. This is fine for the Bob Hope type of comedy (think of him being an unknowing human sacrifice in *Road to Morocco*) but it degrades Groucho's image.

As in *The Cocoanuts*, Groucho is adept at handling the guests over the 'phone. "You've been here six hours and your trunks haven't arrived? Well, put your trousers on and nobody will notice the difference." A would-be guest by the name of Smythe is enraged to the state of apoplexy purely because Groucho sees the spelling of Smith with a 'y' as sheer affectation and goes on to assume everything else about him, like his claim to be married to the woman next to him, to be equally suspect. "You'll hear from me!" bellows Smythe as he withdraws. "Do — if it's only a postcard," replies Groucho sweetly, impervious to his anger. No sooner has Groucho set eyes on the police chief's beard than he reacts with the usual derogatory comment, this time: "I've seen five o'clock shadow but this is ridiculous!" (Another echo of *To Have and Have Not* is to find Dan Seymour playing the same role of a police chief here.)

Groucho is weakened by the superficial quality all his lines have. They aren't the penetrating firecrackers of the old days, but tend to be casual, throw-away lines with no lasting merit. There are also some forced puns such as, on being asked "Will you join me?" by the seductive Beatrice, his reply of, "Why, are you coming apart?"

* * *

Chico leaves most of the punning to Groucho and again plays a fairly straightforward role. But he is back to his crooked ways, rigging prices on his camel taxis. Groucho queries the rates as he takes one. "Don't worry about the price, boss. Whatever you got I take," replies Chico, and we know he can do it. Once again Chico is the hero's devoted friend. Pierre's problem is clearing his name of the charge of collaborating with the enemy by catching Sig Ruman as the wanted Nazi. He is offered information but can't afford to buy it from the informer. He almost takes it by force and the watching Chico comments, "He'll never get anything from that rat without money. That rat is just-a like me." Harpo nods in agreement and Chico collects himself: "Hey, what am I saying?" Harpo wants to pick pockets for the money but Chico surprisingly stops him. Soon afterwards they think of an idea, and fill up the entire dance floor of a club with tables to get tips from queueing visitors. Harpo learns that Ruman has arranged with Beatrice to find her in a compromising position so that he can act the outraged fiancé and shoot Groucho (then he can become manager and look for the treasure which is hidden somewhere in the hotel). This leads to a mimed message scene that parallels the one in *A Day at the Races*. Chico sets out to save Groucho, offering himself as a bodyguard. Groucho asks about his camel business. "In the daytime I'm in the camel business, at night I'm a bodyguard." As in a great many Chico-Groucho conversations, Groucho acts as the obliging feed: "What happens if I get shot during the day?" "I give you a free ride on my camel!" replies Chico, never lost for an answer. "If I'm your bodyguard I'll watch you like a mother watches a baby," he further assures Groucho. "Is the mother pretty?" asks Groucho, taking the same sidetrack with a nurse that Chico took in conversing with Groucho during *Monkey Business*.

Groucho won't give up his rendezvous with Beatrice and arrives at her door with all the prerequisites for a wildly romantic evening: a big bunch of hired roses, champagne, champagne glasses in his pocket. The curtains are drawn, Strauss is on the gramophone. The mood is more that of Mata Hari and World War One, if not reminiscent of Groucho's date with Miss Nora. "Hey, boss, you got a woman in there?" calls Chico just as he did in *A Day at the Races*. Groucho decides they'd be better off in his room but Beatrice tries to delay him for the plan. Speaking in a babyish voice about her dog, she tells him: "But I can't leave Frou-Frou. You wouldn't want me to leave my little poochie-goochie." "I'll meet you halfway," says Groucho, "Bring the poochie and leave the goochie here", in as nonsensical a division of a word as his lazily putting an 'O' of 'O.K.' on a letter in *A Day at the Races* and deferring the 'K' until later. He has enough on his hands but has to add the gramophone in moving down to his room. Chico interrupts again and Groucho wearily shifts back, leaving Ruman to barge into a second empty room brandishing his revolver. When Groucho reaches Bea's room once more, he can't get in. Chico has beaten him to it. For Chico to end up with Bea results in his most positive amorous assertion since *Horse Feathers*. As for Groucho, his great lover image once more fails to be upheld in practice.

A NIGHT IN CASABLANCA: Groucho's wildly romantic evening with Beatrice (Lisette Verea) — a bunch of hired roses, a bucket of champagne....

Chico is really a middleman here with little to do independently of Groucho and Harpo. He gets in a piano piece, of course, which he introduces as "a little classy number — the second movement of the Beer Barrel Polka." It is a deliberate poke at classical music in favour of his own tastes.

* * *

Harpo has nothing to equal the sight gag with the falling building at the start of the film, but manages many appealing moments. He is still apt to follow women and an old trait that is revived is the *recherché* appetite. Chico brings Harpo in to act as a guinea pig for Groucho in case his food is poisoned. He is first thrown bits to catch in his mouth like a performing seal. He silences Groucho's protests at losing his meal by pretending to writhe in agony for a moment. Eating like a maniac, he moves on to a lighted candle, transferring the flame to the end of a finger, chewing off some wax and then replacing the flame. He offers the inkwell to Groucho who declines, then downs the ink himself; finds time to intercept a 'phone-call, after which he replaces the receiver and sprinkles salt over it, enabling Chico to interpret for Harpo as usual by telling Groucho, "Salt Lake City"; takes a cup of coffee from Groucho's hands, swallows it and nibbles at the china; and starts on a vienna loaf with Chico eating from the other end. A hungry Groucho asks us, "Wouldn't it be great if they ate each other up?"

In *The Big Store* Harpo had an ingenious contraption for waking himself up. Typically, involving a weight falling on his head, it was the kind of device that would send the normal person more firmly to sleep. But Harpo isn't normal. Here he has a shoe-cleaning device that is both time-saving and good fun to work. He also has a hinged sole on his shoe for snapping up litter and cigarette ends. He gives one girl his leg (the old trick) and has her worried until she realises his designs are not on her but on her cigarette end.

When the hotel elevator stalls with Groucho and Harpo aboard, Harpo is despatched through the roof to bring assistance. He assumes a look of terror but is pushed out (as in *Duck Soup* and *A Night at the Opera*, the reluctant 'volunteer'). He leans against the wall of the elevator shaft and falls into the secret room housing the Nazi loot. Inside, a scowling cherub on a Rembrandt prompts him to make a gookie for comparison (like the imitative face he makes at a performer on stage in *A Night at the Opera*). He is more attracted to the beautiful woman on a further Rembrandt and when he finds a harp, he starts to play it to her. Cut off from the rest of the world, in an almost timeless setting of historic objects, he is again performing (the second Hungarian Rhapsody) for himself, which means for the dream figure on the canvas. He then folds up the painting inside his shirt (like the Beaugard of *Animal Crackers*), to bring it out eventually as a pin-up (shades of the calendar girl in *Horse Feathers*).

Back in the shaft, Harpo has to get the impatient Groucho out of the elevator. Impressed with the need for urgency, he does the job the quickest way he knows how, swinging an axe at the cable and ropes. Groucho's descent registers on the floor indicator which bounces back a couple of floors before settling. Another such moment of physical punishment comes when Harpo is concealed in the lid of an opened trunk. As the Nazi rests his fingers over the edge of the trunk, Harpo lets his weight bring the lid down.

Harpo is the Nazi's valet and is treated as badly as he was by Lassparri or Morgan, only here he is not playing around or disobeying orders, merely doing his best. He continues to do what he can and when the man loses the toupee that he needs to be seen in public without being recognised, Harpo cheers him up by announcing he has found it. He has had no training in the subtle distinctions between toupees and for him any old mop seems more than adequate. For his efforts he gets called a dog and shaken about by Kurt, one of the Nazi's henchmen. In the face of such bestiality, Harpo preserves his dignity and offers a card. Kurt, who modestly describes himself as the finest swordsman in all Bavaria, is happy to arrange a duel. Swords are produced and Harpo has first choice: being no fool, he takes both. But the duel gets under way and while the Nazi cries out for a little blood ("It will soothe me to see a human being in pain"), Harpo parries every move Kurt makes and leans against the

A NIGHT IN CASABLANCA: Harpo accidentally whisks away the toupee worn by the Nazi (Sig Ruman) while vacuuming the room.

wall yawning as Kurt exhausts himself. The whole scene is the fine demonstration of Harpo's effortless command over a situation. The score is kept by the rings on a curtain rod, as it was during the battle in *Duck Soup*.

* * *

In the hotel's casino, Harpo seems to remain the favoured child of the gods when, naively persisting with the same number at the gambling tables, he breaks the bank. But this leads to him being charged with having rigged the game with Groucho. They, Chico and Pierre end up in jail. This is again the point of despair reached so clearly in the first two M-G-M films but it is much less systematically approached and therefore much weaker. Ruman and his gang are loose, able to search the hotel while the Marx brothers sit around in jail, once again apportioning the blame. Chico and Groucho decide it rests with Harpo who isn't at all pleased at being picked on. They break out of jail in the end (by relatively routine means: comparison with the jail break in *The Cocoanuts* emphasises the loss of imagination over the intervening years).

The following scene where the Marxes creep into Ruman's hotel room as he is packing and unpack his work behind his back is a good one. As they dart to and from their hiding places, the screen puts on display an almost balletic precision of movement backed by split-second timing and complete silence by which they are never quite seen. At the start, just before Ruman comes in, they are alone; then hearing him coming they all look around for hiding places and it is Groucho — as one would expect — who keeps getting shouldered out and rushes around helplessly, only diving into a closet in the nick of time. Ruman's irritation increases as he finds the room in disarray while the way the Marxes co-operate on their sallies forth shows a very gratifying unity of action between the brothers, working again for a common cause. It makes comprehensible and even a little terrifying the mental effect all this has on the Nazi as the world becomes for him an insane nightmare, even more inexplicable than the changes of lay-out that confront the detective in *A Night at the Opera* who at least knows he is in Marx territory and is on his guard. Here the man believes himself to be in safe quarters and has nobody to suspect. In a new way, we find the same kind of disturbing effect the Marxes obtain with their challenge to individuality. Even if the Nazi were quick enough, what would he make of the ghostly form in a white sheet creeping across the room (Harpo under a dust cover)? And when the man hands over a fountain pen to Kurt, who has returned and stands not a foot away, and it disappears *en route* so that Kurt hasn't got it when asked to return it, we see Harpo, as the hidden third party, going a stage further than in even the trouble he caused between the Captain and the First Officer in *Monkey Business*. There, the First Officer knows Harpo is at work and they eventually prove it. Here, quite invisible to the two men, never even suspected behind the white dust cover, he is able to make them both satisfied the other is playing him up. Harpo becomes, in a very credible way, as powerful as the Puck who sowed such mischief in the enchanted wood of *A Midsummer Night's Dream*, while dispensing with supernatural powers and making do with a well-developed talent for mischief.

The climax itself occurs on an aeroplane in which Ruman and his gang are attempting to leave the country. A reformed Beatrice helps the Marx brothers aboard and Harpo soon knocks out the pilot and hopefully settles down at the controls, pulling and pushing levers at random so that the 'plane bounces, slows down, accelerates, and generally alarms everyone. Beatrice hastily revives the pilot but Harpo, as sensitive to crooks as he was in Chico's reconstruction of a crime in *At the Circus*, firmly hits the half-dazed man on the head again. Perhaps he has complete faith in his own abilities to fly the 'plane. From past experience, *we* have at any rate; or as one critic argued it, "You want everything for him, his delights are so simple. I thought it monstrous to let the aeroplane crash when he flew it. The director seems to me to show no understanding of Marxian magic. A 'plane flown by mad Harpo should have the happiest landing." But for once Harpo becomes a cropper; at least (and maybe even deliberately) he crashes the 'plane into police headquarters so that Ruman, his toupee having gone adrift in the shake up, can be recognised as the wanted war criminal and be arrested. The romantic leads at last find some purpose in the film by kissing each other so that Beatrice can rashly observe: "If a thing like that could only happen to me..." A little faster on the move than poor Thelma Todd at the end of *Horse Feathers*, Beatrice flees in panic from a lustful Groucho, Chico and Harpo... a pleasing image with which to end the last full-fledged Marx picture.

A NIGHT IN CASABLANCA: Chico and Harpo hide out in a trunk and drive the Nazi (Sig Ruman) to drink as they disarrange the room while he isn't looking.

15. Love Happy (1949)

In *Love Happy*, Harpo appears as a solitary tramp helping out an impoverished stage company who believe they will have the greatest smash hit since *Showboat*. He is the one who scouts for their food, but when he returns they practically bury him in the rush. However, it is enough for him to receive a smile of gratitude from Maggie, the leading lady, whom he secretly loves.

Clearly this is a very different Harpo from the fellow of past acquaintance. The character is even called Harpo and the real Harpo seems to be indulging a wish to escape from his traditional role and become another sentimental 'little fellow'. He makes a point of comforting Maggie, doing little tricks, bringing out his harp to stop her sobbing (playing 'Swanee River' with strains of the *Love Happy* theme tune). In this scene we see where Harpo lives: in what is apparently a disused shed in Central Park. These humble conditions add to the pathos of his age compared to Maggie's. They show that he is living outside society now that he has come to settle down rather than to be a happy-go-lucky wanderer, an impression that is only belatedly dispelled.

Chico appears as Faustino the Great. "Somebody told me you're putting on a show with unknowns," he tells the producer. "You're hiring-a peoples a-never been heard of. Well, I'm the most unknown and unheard of actor who's never been on Broadway." It turns out that the thing he's most unknown for is mind-reading. After this nice piece of argument, Chico has little to do worth remembering. There are one or two nostalgic references to the past — to Tutsi-Frutsi Ice-Cream (his cry as a race-track tout in *A Day at the Races*) and a few words of mumbled (mock?) Italian (*Horse Feathers*, etc.) He joins the company, happy to work without pay, interprets more of Harpo's messages, and plays the piano prominently.

Groucho's work in *Love Happy* looks more like an afterthought. He functions first as the narrator, telling how as a private detective (Sam Grunion by name) he has been tracking down the royal Romanoff diamonds. "For eleven years I trailed them... through the Khyber Pass, over the Pyrenees, round the Cape of Good Hope, and in the Gimbal's basement." Then he makes a kind of guest appearance within the picture towards the end, part of this involving him fleetingly with Marilyn Monroe in one of her early roles. "Mr. Grunion," she murmurs, "I want you to help me... some men are following me." But Groucho is unable to ditch the plot which has placed him in the hands of a hired killer at this time. Perhaps writer Frank Tashlin was making it up to Groucho when, as the writer-producer-director of *Will Success Spoil Rock Hunter? (Oh For A Man!)*, he brought him on at the end as George Schmidlapp, the secret love of a later sex-bomb, Jayne Mansfield.

Unlike Harpo and Chico, whose appearance is unaltered, Groucho has changed somewhat. The glasses and moustache are now genuine and he looks much older than in *A Night in Casablanca*. On the credit side, he sports a Sherlock Holmes hat that likens him further to some bird of prey as he stalks the rooftops at the end, though accompanied by irritatingly insistent music. Here he meets up with Harpo and the supposedly seductive Madame Egilichi who heads the gang seeking the valuable necklace. When she declares within Harpo's hearing that she would kill anyone with the necklace, Harpo engagingly reverts to his old character and looks out for himself by planting it on Groucho, knowing quite well that he can retrieve it at a more opportune moment. Groucho is as helpless as ever when Harpo is around. He has his problems with Madame Egilichi when he wants to search her for the necklace, much as he contemplated searching Peerless Pauline in *At the Circus*. "If this were a French picture I could do it," he says to us but the effect is tame. There is something rather seedy about Groucho's manner and appearance in *Love Happy*. The same comment applied to Groucho's position at the start of *The Big Store* but there he grew as the picture went on.

Chico also falls under the spell of Madame Egilichi at one point. He promises to do anything for her and she sends him out for sardine tins, hoping that he will return with the one that has the hidden necklace. Chico wholeheartedly declares that if she likes sardines that much he'll cover her in sardines, giving it the sound of a rather lewd proposition. Eventually he returns, pleased at having served her better than she can imagine. He unloads tins of anchovy and can't understand her short-tempered reaction.

We now have to consider Harpo's appearance in more detail for it is essentially his film. He is on screen the most and his talent still shines, if not too brightly, against this rather tawdry backcloth. His manner still has a youthful gaiety and jauntiness about it. His features have become perhaps even more flexible and rubbery with the creases of age and his expressions still make a fascinating study, like the childish scowl on his face when he's pushed around as part of a stage number. The moments of intended pathos are unsuccessful because we feel no concern for Maggie. In fact, we care rather more for Rosa in *A Night at the Opera* or Judy in *A Day at the Races* who really had something to cry about and put a brave face on it. Harpo's big sequences suffer from too many effects with speeded film and other obvious trick work.

He's first seen on the sidewalk outside a delicatessen, helping customers as they leave, carrying their baskets or lighting a cigarette with a blow-lamp attachment that works through the flower in his buttonhole (reminiscent of the actual blow-lamp he had in *Duck Soup*). He is a'so quickly passing foodstuffs into his raincoat pocket. Only a small dog is wise enough to see through him and, maintaining the traditional antipathy between dogs and Harpo, yaps to gain attention. Harpo gets his revenge by showing it a 'gookie' through the car window, making it scuttle with terror under a rug.

In the basement of the delicatessen, Harpo makes a quick foray and removes the sardine tin in which the Romanoff diamonds are being delivered to Madame Egilichi. Eventually, Harpo is caught and searched for the sardine tin. Madame Egilichi entrances him with her physical charms — his face sets in suspended dubiousness, mouth half-open, eyes fixed on her. One would like to think that he is playing up to her and can't be so easily won over; but she does seem to have an easy hold over him, if only sexually. In fact Harpo's mind is so much on her that when he's struck by her henchmen he hits back, then waves at her, having removed the distraction. While this goes on, the pockets of his old raincoat are emptied and a mountain of junk slowly piles up. It includes a 'welcome' mat, a pair of legs from a shop-window mannequin, a rotating barber's pole, a block of ice (from *Horse Feathers,* no doubt), a postal delivery box marked "Moss Kaufman" (i.e. George S. Kaufman and Moss Hart), a live dog, and so on. Unfortunately the joke is flattened by its excessive length: it would have been far better to have upended Harpo and on a cut to close-up arranged for it all to fall out at once. Additionally, as Harpo is pressed to the wall being searched, so much time passes that we start to suspect that the items brought forth are really being pulled through the wall. It is essential that we shouldn't start to question Harpo's ability to carry it all around. Actually, the· range of things he carried was better established in earlier films when he produced a candle lit at both ends or a steam-

LOVE HAPPY:
Chico tells Madame Egilichi that, if she wants sardines, he'll smother her in sardines.

ing cup of coffee in one swift move. They carried the suggestion that there was no limit to what he had, whereas in *Love Happy* a definite limit is reached when Harpo has nothing more.

The gang are forced to set about torturing Harpo. One feels he ought to disconcert them by enjoying their attentions but he comes to look rather upset (even so his miserable expression has something witty about it, like every Harpo face). He soon suffers an ordeal on William Tell lines and there is a delightful moment when he snatches the apple off his head and ravenously bites into it. He grabs the gun waved in front of him and threatens to drill a hole in his head if they don't let him finish eating. He pulls the trigger a couple of times to show that he means it. There are empty clicks and the gang start forward. But like the gun in *Go West* which was first a gun, then a clothes-brush, then a real, loaded gun, this one goes off when Harpo moves it away from his head and live bullets fly out. After it should be empty, Harpo manages to get a couple more shots out of it than the makers intended.

Later Maggie is grabbed by the gang in her dressing room. Harpo realises what is going on but, lacking his old resourcefulness, simply runs off to fetch help. It does at least lead to a good message scene with Chico, Harpo doing his quick charades and Chico some inspired guessing, egged on by whistles of encouragement. Drastically simplified, it runs in part like this: Harpo outlines a dog. Chico wonders if it's a St. Bernard. No. An even bigger dog? A Great Dane? Yes. Harpo touches his face. Great Dane got a dimple? Whiskers? Jaw? Yes. Great Dane — jaw. Great danger! Harpo gets down on his knees like Al Jolson doing "Mammy". Chico keeps repeating "Mammy", Harpo half-stopping it on his lips. Ma- Ma- Ma-. Then Harpo turns a key in an imaginary door. Ma-key. Maggie! Harpo whistles congratulations and goes on to spell out that Madame Egilichi is going to murder Maggie. As has been mentioned before, this new derivation of words make us realise that these are just combinations of sounds with different meanings, though amazingly flexible as they are separated and reassembled into new words.

The climax of the film is the chase over the rooftops and up and

LOVE HAPPY:
Rooftop finale,
with Madame Egilichi,
Groucho and Harpo.

down the neon signs of New York. It is moderately but not memorably amusing. Besides Harpo's use of Groucho, a couple of old tricks emerge: the habit of giving his leg (Groucho receiving it) and the appearance of one of the mannequin's legs, adding one more to the collection of false limbs that have decorated Harpo's career. Here, too, we find Harpo joining up with a horse once more. It is the winged horse of the Mobilgas neon sign and Harpo rides it to get away from the gangsters below. More than a horse, it is Pegasus, the steed of the Muses; after all his years of service to Thalia, the muse of comedy, he deserves her helping hand.

The parts of Harpo's performance that linger most vividly are several sight gags that have a cartoon quality linking them all most probably to Tashlin. Told by Chico, who is trying to read his mind, that he should clear his head, Harpo inserts a handkerchief in one ear and pulls it out of the other, then runs it back and forth. He staggers out of a neon sign that puffs smoke in its promotion of Kool cigarettes, and not only, as he presses his stomach, does the smoke come out of his mouth but also out of his ears. He brushes his hair in a mirror, then turns the mirror over to see the back of his head reflected as he brushes that.

Harpo does each of these very well. They are quite convincingly executed. But they amuse us less as insights into Harpo's character than as clever technical achievements more befitting a magician's act. There is another one that cries to be drawn and doesn't come off: when Harpo produces a tablecloth with all the plates and cutlery laid out on it. It just can't be done smoothly enough — the cloth

LOVE HAPPY: Groucho as the private eye Sam Grunion.

LOVE HAPPY: Climactic chase — Harpo presses his stomach and out comes the smoke he has absorbed from the neon sign, as Throckmorton (Melville Cooper) attempts to recover the diamond necklace.

should be as smooth as a magic carpet and not crumple under the weight of the attached props.

*　　*　　*

How, then, do the Marxes finish their screen career? Chico very surprisingly ends up in Groucho's office, playing cards with a large dog with the outcome that he loses his jacket to the animal. It is apt that there should be this final evidence that he is no match in intelligence for even dumb animals. He is also allowed a streak of his old stubbornness when he won't answer Groucho's telephone for him. The surprise is that he shouldn't have gone off with his old pal, Harpo.

Groucho ends up seeming very content to be the latest husband of Madame Egilichi, but it is sad to watch him allowing himself to be henpecked over the telephone by her.

Harpo at least — and it *is* his film — departs in a fitting manner. He doesn't get the girl, but it was obvious that he never would as she is in love with someone younger. He does, however, carry off the royal Romanoff diamonds. The show is a success, Maggie is happy, and he can move on. Throwing aside the humble abode (which, it seems in the end, was only temporary while he helped Maggie), he makes off into the darkness beyond the neon signs, dancing a little jig, like Puck "a merry wanderer of the night." The diamond necklace is the souvenir of his adventures; it has no further value for him as he is unaware of its true worth.

16. The Fifties

About the time of *Love Happy*, Groucho became involved in a series called *You Bet Your Life* which went out over both radio and television, winning several professional awards. Though built to a quiz format, its point of appeal was entirely Groucho, ad-libbing and sometimes reviving lines from his movies in questioning the participants. Here Groucho decisively abandoned the old screen image to become a friendly, avuncular figure, if with a roguish eye for the prettier guests.

Harpo and Chico did miscellaneous work. Besides playing piano and doing comedy on shows for television, Chico even turned up in a Playhouse 90 drama. Harpo brought many of his old tricks to variety shows as well as the old unquenchable spirit. On a Milton Berle show (January 14, 1959), he was questioned about his late arrival by Uncle Miltie and described a vertical in-and-out shape. Uncle Miltie asked if Harpo could get him one and didn't exactly have in mind the Coke bottle Harpo brought back. Along with this echo of past mime scenes, Harpo gave his leg to the host, played around hungrily during a Kraft recipe commercial, and made faces through his harp that had a studio audience roaring while Berle was on camera. There was no sign of Lucille Ball's special talent for comedy in *Room Service*, but Harpo, guesting nearly twenty years later with her at the height of *I Love Lucy's* popularity, made a memorable partner for her. "His scenes with Lucille provided one of the best comic half-hours on American television that season — not to mention a glimpse of the might-have-been. Lucy, on a visit to Hollywood where husband Ricky (Desi Arnaz) is making a film, encounters Harpo in her hotel room. Bent on seducing her, he gives frantic chase, and the fun is on. It could have been chaos, but rarely have two clowns shown such rapport and timing in a television performance. All the Harpoisms are there: the shake-a-leg, horn honking, horrendous leers, and in one superb highlight the old mirror gag, with Lucy mimicking Harpo's expressions and movements perfectly until the inevitable slip-up which sets the insanity in motion again. The two complement each other perfectly, though Harpo assumes complete command" (Ted Gilling).

They were all still around, carrying on with their life's work of entertaining, and if the material was either over-familiar or unworthy of them, it was made more than tolerable by the fund of goodwill from old memories, and the sheer pleasure of seeing them again. Apart from this American work, the world audience saw Groucho in

164

several undistinguished movies, and all three brothers in separate episodes of *The Story of Mankind*, a curiosity of a film released in 1957. Groucho was saddled with poor dialogue as the Dutchman who conned Manhattan Island from the Indians; Chico was rather forgettable as a monk advising Columbus; but Harpo was magnificent as Isaac Newton, quietly playing his harp in an orchard when a falling apple gives him the Great Idea.

On at least one occasion the Marxes reappeared together, if only for a moment. This was a teleplay in the G. E. Theater series called *The Incredible Jewel Robbery* and shown on March 8, 1959. Harpo and Chico starred and Groucho guested (unbilled due to his contract with another network). Although far from successful, the production had a couple of marvellous flashes. In pantomime (with music on the soundtrack) Chico and Harpo broke into shops stealing the equipment to disguise an automobile as a police car — all rather tedious and not funny. Then, outside a jeweller's shop selected from a stolen telephone directory, Harpo donned a disguise, including a Sherlock Holmes cap, with his back to the camera. As he turned, the show suddenly came to life: Harpo had put on a one-piece pair of glasses with attached eyebrows, a fake rectangular moustache, a cigar, and become Groucho! He paced up and down the pavement with mischievous alacrity, exactly catching Groucho's walk, before going in to hold up the store. Chico then came along as the policeman to 'arrest' him. They fled but had to pick up a woman outside a deaf and dumb home (preserving the ban on words) and deliver her to the maternity hospital. Eventually caught (though not by any imaginative twist of writing), they were put into a line-up at the police station. Chico was identified as the 'policeman' but Harpo escaped through not being in disguise. Then suddenly and for no reason Groucho entered and loped up and down the line, cigar in hand. He was picked out as the hold-up man. Then, as Harpo and Chico dashed to his side and Harpo handed over his leg, Groucho spoke the first and last line of the film: "We won't talk until we see our lawyer." Down came the little wooden puppet used on *You Bet Your Life* with the words 'The End' on it. It was impossible not to feel that the makers were relying on the name of the Marxes to carry thin and routine material. But despite this, it was a pleasure to see them giving assured performances, looking young and fresh enough to make another feature film, so that Billy Wilder's scheme (see Chapter 14) didn't seem at all fanciful when it came along.

Now, sadly, Chico and Harpo have gone, in order of seniority; and Margaret Dumont, too. But Groucho continues, making a series of shows for British television in 1965 and recalling how he did a live skit with Margaret just before she died. It is surely a marvellous show-business saga — more than fifty years of tussling with an audience for laughs.

17. Trends and Traditions

Having finished this commentary on the Marx Brothers' world of comedy, it seems appropriate to consider in what ways it is unique and to what extent it fits in with other work.

The Marxes must have owed their skill as performers to their vaudeville experience and we know that Harpo evolved many of his tricks on the road. Their basic appearances were determined at this time, but their material must have changed when they were using scripts provided by outside writers (though Kalmar and Ruby were 'insiders' with a vaudeville background and we have suggested that their writing was at a more popular level than that of, say, Perelman with a literary background). It is difficult to establish how much their routines had in common with vaudeville comedy of that time, since the latter was worked out before audiences, and little of it has been recorded in any detail. One apparently famous routine that originated in 1906 and became a complete act a few years later has been recently printed under the title *Dr. Kronkhite — a Vaudeville Classic*.[27] It starred Charlie Dale as the doctor and Joe Smith as Mr. Dubious, his patient. Two points become evident from a reading of it, and these match the general impression given of vaudeville and music-hall humour by other sources. First, the skit continually invites laughter at stupidity. There is an air of futility and pointlessness about the whole routine. In this respect, it makes one think of Chico and he probably has the closest link with vaudeville. Harpo of course was also relentlessly stupid in his 'idiot boy' days, but he became both a clown in a broader circus tradition, and a distinct character with certain set ways and routines. The Smith-Dale skit has nothing of Groucho's 'offbeat' intelligence or mental agility, and he was more a precursor of the radio wits of the thirties, a slickly contemporary and sharply defined character. The stupidity of vaudeville humour must have been accompanied by smuttiness but this is not seen in the skit, and is very faint in the Marx films (even then it is almost never objectionable: the hidden meaning of Groucho's name S. Quentin Quale in *Go West* is the only doubtful case, although the term "darkies" from a song lyric is now regrettable in *Duck Soup*).

The second observation prompted by *Dr. Kronkhite* is that, while the crosstalk is slick enough, it keeps stopping and starting. The skit is really set up for a number of separate gags and smart comebacks. It could almost be Chico saying to the nurse "I'll wait"; the nurse replies to the patient: "Take a chair, please." "Thank you, I'll take it on my way out... what's the doctor's office hours?"

"They're from 12 to 3 . . . 3 to 6 . . . 6 to 9 . . . 9 to 12 . . . and 12 to 3." "He gives good odds, he must be a horse doctor." When the doctor engages the patient, a fair amount of the European dialect humour emerges, though not consistently as it does, in a trumped up way, with Chico (it relates to the inflow of European immigrants and is a definite stage in vaudeville humour which Chico clearly represents). In the skit, for instance, the letters T.V. mean Tuesday and Vendsday; a doctor whò practised in Cairo is a chiropracticer; and the "weal I eat" is veal. It is a moderately funny piece, but it lacks the consistent and sustained style of a Groucho-Chico encounter. In particular, the characters are not clearly defined like Groucho and Chico. It can only work at a more superficial level.

The Marxes are reputed to have improvised wildly and strayed from their material, but they had a written script to stray from and return to that gave form to their work. (In many respects, Spike Milligan's great hit, *Son of Oblomov,* derived from a respectable stage original, seems to occupy a similar place on the London stage to the Marx shows of the twenties.) However good the Marxes were at finding their own material, they were not able to steer their scripts back on course when less expert writers than Kaufman, Ryskind, Kalmar and Ruby, etc., were working for them.

These expert writers, of course, were part of a rich outcrop of American humorous writing — Robert Benchley and Ring Lardner

Left, Harpo (A NIGHT AT THE OPERA).
Right, Groucho (THE BIG STORE).

come to mind immediately. This is undoubtedly a tradition that the Marx films follow. We can ponder if in a wider sense, the Marxes owe anything to Edward Lear and Lewis Carroll, who are popularly likened to the team. (There is a direct reference to Carroll in *Animal Crackers*, Groucho finishing a series of remarks to Mrs. Rittenhouse with the words: "And now, madam, the time has come as the walrus said to speak of . . ." It is just a friendly quotation that must strike a responsive chord in many spectators).

Carroll and Lear were both Victorians, conjuring up worlds of fantasy to amuse children — gentle places full of eccentricities and inventions, essentially harmless. Lear adds new words, new places, new creatures to inhabit his realm of the imagination. The wonderland of Alice is a dream world where the impossible can be properly impossible, not subject to any logic, where anything can happen and everything can be left behind on awakening. Alice and the reader of Lear retain their sanity; it is the other world that is insane.

The Marx Brothers comedies are the reverse of this. The settings have a kind of abstraction (the *haut monde* of the first two films particularly) but they do pass for a real period and have recognisable affinities with life at the time. Helped by many topical allusions and familiar preoccupations, we can lazily accept it as real. The Marx capers derive their strength from contrasting with this monotonously sane, pompously narrow and petty-minded background, and their madness is real, not for dreams.

Any similarities aside, there is a real difference in tone. Alice's adventures are mildly bewildering, the Marxes sharply lucid. The rudeness, vulgarity and exuberance of the Marx outlook is not matched in Lear or Carroll.

* * *

An obvious direct influence must have been the silent cinema. The Marxes have often gone on record over their respect for Chaplin. Harpo writes of his vaudeville days: "Lately, on the road, I had been seeing lots of movies. But Fairbanks I only saw if I couldn't find a Chaplin picture playing anywhere. Charlie Chaplin was my idea of comic genius. I would watch a Chaplin picture four, five or six times over. What an artist!" [14]

But the Marx Brothers still evolved a particular style that has no direct ancestry. There are certain parallels of style and situation. The 'mirror image' routine of *Duck Soup* — though without the extra twist of *three* Grouchos on the loose — was something of a staple in vaudeville (with the Schwartz Brothers particularly) and silent movies (e.g., Max Linder's *Seven Years Bad Luck*, 1921, and — it is said — Chaplin's *The Floorwalker*). It pops up again after the Marxes' use of it with Abbott and Costello, and with Red Skelton on American television (Skelton is perhaps the only interesting successor to Harpo in the line of individualised clowns, although with a quite different character). Then the climax to *A Night at the Opera* is sometimes said to have been inspired by the similar imbroglio that ends René Clair's *Le Million*. Also, others have taken over gags originated by the Marx Brothers. Groucho throws away a cigarette lighter like a used match, just as Jacques Tati does twenty-five years later in *Mon Oncle*. Bob Hope with his eyes shut mistakenly switches partners from Hedy Lamarr to his man-servant while dancing in *My Favorite Spy* rather as Groucho ends up with Alky Briggs in *Monkey Business*. In *Son of Oblomov*, Spike Milligan clings to the rising curtain as Harpo once did in vaudeville (and others probably before him). Certainly Tati's brilliance is not impaired by what is either a relatively trifling coincidence or an unconscious borrowing. Greater parallels like the mirror scenes are unimportant, too. One doesn't group Linder and the Marx Bros. together because of it. The important points are that the Marxes did an enormous amount that was fresh and distinctive, and that all their work is supported by an attitude that comes from their particular characters. With shallow performers, all the fun would lie in the technical handling of the scene, but with the Marxes the scene is backed by all that the Marxes have established at other times, like Harpo's traditional mastery of Groucho. The comedians are still different when the comedy itself is not.

* * *

If the Marxes, with Fields and Mae West, were matching the mood of the Depression, there might well be a similarity of tone and considerable comic merit in other films of the time. After all, the same writers who served the Marx Brothers were busy writing for other comedians. Naturally, their approach would have been conditioned by the style and capabilities of these other performers but something of the same inventiveness and comic attitude ought to be there. However, it is not surprising that a film like Eddie Cantor's *Roman Scandals*, involving no less than six Marx writers (although Kalmar and Ruby did only music and lyrics for it — Kaufman co-wrote the story while George Oppenheimer, Arthur Sheekman and Nat Perrin provided additional material), should still be rather mild and conventional, if lavish and entertaining, because Samuel Goldwyn is the conventionally-minded kind of producer whose taste would not have allowed otherwise. Kalmar and Ruby also did work as two of the three scenarists on Cantor's *The Kid from Spain* (1932) while Morrie Ryskind is credited on Cantor's *Palmy Days* a year earlier.

A more promising field of study looks like the work of (Bert) Wheeler and (Robert) Woolsey, an ex-vaudeville team, on the one hand said to have "afflicted the screen for five years with wheezy vaudeville gags" (Griffith and Mayer), on the other to be dated but still amusing (*Bantam TV Movie Almanac and Ratings*). It is certainly hard to imagine that *Kentucky Kernels* has nothing of interest when Kalmar and Ruby wrote it a year after *Duck Soup*. The pair, ex-vaudeville themselves, also wrote Wheeler and Woolsey's *The Cuckoos* (1930). S. J. Perelman worked on their *Hold 'Em Jail* (1932) which had a crazy football game that might be comparable to that of *Horse Feathers*. *The Nitwits* (1935) credits Al Boasberg as a writer, the same year in which he devised gags for *A Night at the Opera*.

Kalmar and Ruby also worked for Joe E. Brown on at least two farces, *Broadminded* (1931) and *Bright Lights* (1935), on each side of their work for the Marx Brothers. S. J. Perelman was a scenarist on Jack Oakie's *Sitting Pretty* (1933) which has satirical and madhouse episodes that ought to have offered Perelman scope. It is these and other films of this period — which must have been much freer than the better-known, big budget films — that will have to be investigated if the Marx Brothers' place in film comedy is to be fully determined.

1933, the year of *Duck Soup*, represented the depth of the Depression; in 1934, with the New Deal, a more optimistic era was ushered in and the style of comedy began to alter. There was the private world of harmless eccentricities unearthed by the screwball comedies; there was Shirley Temple; and there was the more purposeful air of Frank Capra's social comedies. Public taste seems to have drastically changed and the Marx Brothers probably had to change with it to go on — as in fact they did at M-G-M from 1935. The early Marx films may have partly been a response to the period, but the Marxes were lucky to find their individual form of humour so widely acceptable.

*   *   *

Salvador Dali was a great admirer of the Marxes and considered their films to be surrealism applied to the cinema (they modestly settled for the term 'lunatic comedy'; they have never admitted to anything more profound in their work). He brought Harpo a harp with barbed-wire strings and spoons and forks for tuning knobs; he also wrote a script for the team but it was never filmed, of course.[19]

The Surrealist Movement developed about the time the Marxes' film career did, and the International Surrealist Exhibition of 1936 was labelled by one London newspaper 'The Marx Brothers of art'. There are certainly parallels between comedy and surrealism and between it and the Marx Brothers in particular. As James Feibleman observes: "The classic method of comedy is evident in the technique of the surrealists. The juxtaposition of objects and hence of relations which do not seem to have any good reason for belonging together lies at the bottom of all the surrealists' work." [20] This was not only a visual movement of course, and the technique applied to words and thoughts (dissociated thinking) as by André Breton is paralleled by Groucho's work. In general, the surrealists were able to exploit the element of incongruity even further than most screen comedy — the cartoon was generally not daring enough to go as far as it might have done, and flesh-and-blood performers had their limitations. But in Groucho's dialogue and Harpo's brilliance as a clown (especially the Punch and Judy scene in *Monkey Business,* all in all the most surrealistic of the Marx films), the pair were able to confuse our senses — what we heard and saw didn't make sense and yet it did — it *was* happening and it did have some kind of logic on a different plane — perhaps of the 'superior reality'. André Breton, one of the movement's leaders, said: "Surrealism rests in the belief of the superior reality of certain forms of association neglected heretofore; in the omnipotence of the dream and in the disinterested play of thought". Whether Breton's claim that this is a method for the solution of the principal problems of life can be upheld for surrealism or for the Marx Brothers is more questionable, but the Marxes' comedy is certainly constructive in the sense that the distortion of ordinary reality makes us more aware of what it is; the eyesight and hearing are sharpened to images and words we have come to take for granted.

*   *   *

More recently the Marx Brothers have been connected with the appearance of a theatrical movement commonly termed 'The Theatre of the Absurd'. Again this is a movement that ties in with traditional comedy. Martin Esslin remarks that, in its rebellion against the conventions of the theatre, it confused the theatregoer, but in a music hall "he will find the equally nonsensical cross-talk of the comedian and his stooge, which is equally devoid of plot or narrative content [as the theatre], perfectly acceptable." [28] This is true of the Dr. Kronkhite sketch, and of the Marx Brothers, though they are more real, more accessible than the usual music hall comics or the characters in this genre of plays. In the case of the Marxes, the general audience probably accepted quite readily what the more thoughtful spectator stopped to ponder over.

The Theatre of the Absurd represents a "turning away from language as an instrument for the expression of the deepest levels of meaning." [28] The Marxes were certainly earlier exponents of the 'anti-literary attitude' of the movement as well as the anti-literal one of the surrealists. The team's work is perhaps more valuable for having reached so much larger an audience.

Ionesco has spoken of the three Marx Brothers as being the three biggest influences on his work, and Esslin speaks of the crowded cabin scene of *A Night at the Opera* as having "all the mad proliferation and frenzy of Ionesco."

At times the Marxes go further than most of the Theatre of the Absurd, beyond its sense of the lack of purpose and meaninglessness of life, facts which they take for granted, to throw doubts on the one thing the individual is most certain of: his own identity, his own individuality. This basic assumption is continually challenged, as many examples picked up in this book have shown (there are quite a few more). Then there is a startling forcefulness and persuasiveness about the Marxes work — they are decisive and sure of themselves — that sometimes eludes the Theatre of the Absurd. which has not been so successful with the public nor so immediately rewarding.

*　　*　　*

Yet the Marx Brothers have grown out of date. American society came to resemble a Marx Brothers' world of comedy. Richard Rovere's study of the infamous Senator McCarthy reads like the script of an unfilmed Marx epic. Consider this definition of McCarthyism: ". . . McCarthyism was, among other things, but perhaps foremost among them, a headlong flight from reality. It elevated the ridiculous and ridiculed the important. It outraged common sense and held common sense to be outrageous. It confused the categories of form and value. It made sages out of screwballs and accused wise men of being fools." [35] A perfect description of comedy's Marxism. McCarthy, instead of being laughed into obscurity, was able to get away with it for too long — whereas the screen Groucho picked deserving targets and had no real purpose, influence or ambition, even if his activities in *Duck Soup* are an object lesson in the dangers of demagoguery. McCarthy mentioned a string of facts and people obligingly figured out the association; he even got to the supreme peak of labelling one of his allegedly Communist victims a really important example just because he wasn't a Communist (it's as meaningless as that). He did not of course let anyone pin him down to the mere literal meaning of any verbiage. "I make accusations, I don't answer them," he said. Richard Rovere must forgive anyone seeing Groucho when, faced with exposure at one Committee, he had it adjourned to really amass the evidence. "The morning came. McCarthy showed up, briefcase in hand. Rumpled and breathless, he explained to the Committee that he was all ready with his case, but that something terribly important had come up — a Senate debate on housing. He high-tailed it for the door." And there in *A Day at the Races* is Groucho being pressed for evidence as to his medical credentials confiding that something terribly important happened to him during the 'flu epidemic — he caught the 'flu — and high-tailing it to the nearby racetrack. What is more, the McCarthy entourage included characters with names like Urban P. Van Susteren and Otis Gomillion that sound like nothing more than borrowed Groucho aliases. McCarthy's instant divorces from his Wisconsin judge's seat, his campaign slogan of 'Congress Needs a Tail-Gunner' (which he hadn't been), his absolute failure to uncover any corruption at all, his fundamental attachment to dishonesty even when honesty would have served him better, his unconcerned misreading of ghosted speeches, indeed all his giddy inventions and contradictions seem like echoes from some half-forgotten Marx film. They are so incredible that they are delightful — McCarthy comes over as instinctively likeable and only rationally detestable.

The Marxes couldn't compete with this. Only recently have the satirists really come to grips with the post-atomic bomb era; and to communicate with their audiences, they have had to go further than before — to obscenities, jokes about unmentionable topics and people — or to take the risk of not communicating with the public at all in abstract plays. They have abandoned all discipline (as did also the crazy humour of *The Goon Show*, and as does Spike Milligan today) or (in the plays of the Absurd) taken on almost too much discipline. The Marxes stopped short of all this. (Harpo in 1963 was quoted: "I've nothing against the humor of the age, except that it isn't my humor.") They would have respected Gilbert Highet's judgement on the limits of satire: "Some villainies are too awful for us to despise. We can only shudder at them, and in horror turn away — or try to write a tragedy. Against such crimes, satire is almost impotent. Against all lesser crimes and against all follies, it is a powerful weapon." [31]

18. Conclusion

The work of the Marx Brothers, taking either their best films or their work as a whole, is a modern burlesque epic. Their actions meet all the requirements of the form which is "like a powerfully muscled boor carrying a cudgel and riding a donkey. He is strong enough, perhaps, to accomplish bold deeds of derring-do, but he will not, because he has no style, no inner harmony, no ideals. Whatever he attempts will be graceless and absurd." Marx comedy is low, even puerile, full of vulgar words and images, topical references, simple and direct actions. It lacks the affectations and pretences of mock-heroic parody.

The team's *oeuvre* not only suits the genre but it exactly corresponds to a past classic which mirrored a world that was "taut, narrow, pyramidal, authoritarian, and unintelligent." These traits are certainly part of the world the Marx films set up and the Marx Brothers knock down; but the world in question was the Middle Ages, the work in question the story of Reynard the Fox. In this satire, the king, barons and subjects are represented by different animals. Gilbert Highet describes the balance: "Over against them all stands Reynard the Fox. They are society; he is anti-social. They are rich and powerful; he is clever. They are orthodox and gullible and polite; he is unorthodox and inventive and rude. Reynard the Fox thinks the entire system is absurd, and so he lives the life of an active satirist, exposing it and showing its folly. Once, after twenty glasses of wine, he sings out what he really believes." What he sings after twenty glasses of wine is pretty much what Groucho offers as his philosophy of life in *Horse Feathers* when told that the learned professors have something to tell him. He breaks into song: "I don't know what they have to say / It makes no difference anyway / Whatever it is, I'm against it." Similarly, Groucho could have also sung the words of Brer Fox (as expressed in F. S. Ellis' verse adaptation of 1894, quoted by Highet[31]): "Ever since I was born, I I've felt bitter scorn / For worthy respectable people; / So with a merry heart sing / Here's a fig for the King; / Nought care I for law, crown, or steeple. / 'Tis my honest belief / An industrious thief / Is a blessing to all good society; / To the humdrumming round, / Wherein most men are bound, / He furnishes pleasant variety."

Satire is a mixture of amusement and contempt. In the Marx com-

174

edies, the amusement is much stronger than the derision or, bitterness. These films are far from astringent and are not really attempting to be constructive. They are however fully in line with the American ideal of self-advancement. Their optimism, clear-sightedness, resourcefulness and enthusiasm are worthwhile qualities. Others, like compassion and understanding, are rather lacking but the Marxes are in a way redressing the balance for all the times they have been insisted on (as in comedies with 'heart'). It is an under-displayed side of their character but the Marxes can be at peace (as with the negroes in *A Day at the Races* or in the hold of the ship in *Monkey Business*).

Perhaps the Marxes' finest quality is their underlying purity or innocence. They have no permanent truck with this base world of ours, full of menial considerations, dull routines, and comfortable conformism. Groucho, the apparent 'insider', merely dresses for the part and never follows it through. They oppose education, culture and all forms of regulation as destroying the natural life and man's innate dignity. They are first citizens of a new world, Wilde's "state republican where everyman's a king."

Their example is the more valuable today in a world where pessimism and lack of direction are rife, and comedians find it difficult to bring us cheer and hope even for ordinary living. The case of Jacques Tati sums it up. His work goes from the reckless *joie de vivre* of village life in *Jour de Fête* through the more deliberative air of M. Hulot's exploits at a seaside resort in *Les Vacances de M. Hulot* to the glum picture of modern life in *Mon Oncle* where Hulot is fighting a rearguard action against the times, introducing one or two crazy eccentricities (like tricking people into walking into lamp-posts, which he learns from children) but ultimately despairing. The world looms larger than Tati. Chaplin was one of the first, in *Modern Times*, to recognise the impersonality of the threat to happiness (the Marxes always dealt with people).

The title of this book carries the rather over-worked phrase 'world of comedy'. But only because the Marx Brothers did create *their* world of comedy wherever they went and (never in their key work) submitted to the world they found. They re-ordered things that affected them to their own liking with their own good taste, never pausing to take stock. They were characters in line with an observation made by that veteran cynic of their times, H. L. Mencken, in the fourth series of his *Prejudices:* "The liberation of the human mind has never been furthered by . . . dunderheads; it has been furthered by gay fellows who heaved dead cats into sanctuaries and then went roistering down the highways of the world, proving to all men that doubt, after all, was safe . . . One horse-laugh is worth ten thousand syllogisms. It is not only more effective; it is also vastly more intelligent."

175

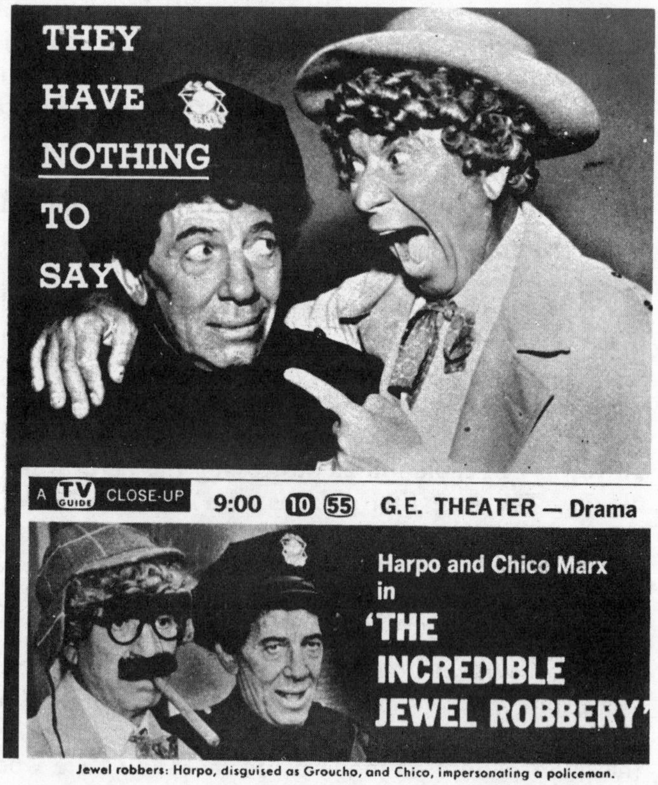
THEY
HAVE
NOTHING
TO
SAY
A TV GUIDE CLOSE-UP
9:00 10 55 G.E. THEATER — Drama
Harpo and Chico Marx
in
'THE
INCREDIBLE
JEWEL ROBBERY'

Jewel robbers: Harpo, disguised as Groucho, and Chico, impersonating a policeman.

Below, CURTAIN CALL: Zeppo, Groucho, Chico, Gummo, and Harpo

Appendix I

MARGARET DUMONT

She was born in 1889 or 1890, was originally a singer, later appeared with George M. Cohan and toured Europe, and was first associated with the Marx Brothers in the stage show *The Cocoanuts*. "I was told that they needed an actress with dignity and poise, to lend legitimate dramatic balance to their comedy. After three weeks as Groucho's leading lady, I nearly had a nervous breakdown. He pushed me about, pulled chairs from under me, broiled steaks in the fireplace of my apartment, put frogs in my bath, and made my life miserable on the stage and off. But I don't regret a minute of it. I just love those boys."

In London (1965) Groucho told an audience: "You know, the curious thing about Margaret, in all the years we played together she never seemed to vary. She was always the austere, dignified dowager that we presented in the pictures. She was the same off the stage as she was on. That was part of her charm. She actually didn't understand any of the jokes. I'm serious — she really didn't understand the jokes. Very seldom. I know there was a joke in *Duck Soup* which was at the finish of the picture. It was a kind of a war and we were in a small cottage — Margaret and myself. She said to me, "What are you doing, Rufus?" I said, "I'm fighting for your honour which is more than you ever did." And later she asked me what did I mean by that."

She made these other films without the Marx Brothers:

1932: *The Girl Habit* (as Mrs. Ledyard). 1934: *Fifteen Wives; Gridiron Flash*.

1935: *The Man With the Electric Voice* (as Sybilla Crum); *Luck of the Game* (as Mrs. Fields). 1936: *Anything Goes* (as Mrs. Wentworth); *Song and Dance Man* (as Mrs. Whitney). 1938: *The Life of the Party* (as Mrs. Penner); *High Flyers; Wise Girl* (as Mrs. Bell-Rivington); *Youth on Parole* (as the Landlady). 1939: *Dramatic School* (as the Pantomimic Teacher)

1941: *For Beauty's Sake*. 1942: *Never Give A Sucker An Even Break* (with W. C. Fields, as Mrs. Hemoglobin); *Born to Sing* (as Mrs. E. V. Lawson); *Sing Your Worries Away* (as Flo Faulkener);

About Face (as Mrs. Culpepper). 1943: *Rhythm Parade* (as Ophelia); *Dancing Masters* (with Laurel and Hardy, as Mrs. Harron). 1944: *Up In Arms* (with Danny Kaye, as Mrs. Willoughby); *Bathing Beauty* (as Mrs. Allenwood); *Seven Days Ashore* (as Mrs. Croxton-Lynch)

1945: *The Horn Blows At Midnight* (with Jack Benny, as Miss Rodholder); *Diamond Horseshoe* (as Mrs. Standish). 1946: *Little Giant (On the Carpet)* (with Abbott and Costello, as Mrs. Hendrickson); *Susie Steps Out* (as Mrs. Starr)

1952: *Stop, You're Killing Me* (as Mrs. Whitelaw); *Three for Bedroom C* (as Mrs. Hawthorne). 1956: *Shake, Rattle and Rock* (as Georgianna). 1959: *Auntie Mame* (uncredited)

1962: *Zotz* (as Persephone Updike). 1965: *What A Way to Go!* (as Mrs. Foster).

Despite failing health, she was active in a variety of roles in her last years, mainly on television with Bob Hope, Dean Martin and others. Just a few days before her death of a heart attack in Hollywood (on March 6, 1965), she had done a TV sketch with Groucho.

"There ought to be a statue erected, or a Congressional Medal awarded, or a national holiday proclaimed, to honour that great woman, Margaret Dumont, the dame who takes the raps from the Marx Brothers . . . a lady of epic ability to take it . . . her fortitude is nothing human. It's godlike." (Cecilia Ager, 1937).

Appendix II

A. Marx Brothers' Major Film Work

THE COCOANUTS. 1929. *A* Paramount *picture.* Monta Bell *in charge of production. Producer:* Walter Wanger. *Associate producer:* James R. Cowan. *Directors:* Robert Florey and Joseph Santley. *Adaptor:* Morrie Ryskind. *Based on the musical play, book by:* George S. Kaufman and Morrie Ryskind. *Music and lyrics:* Irving Berlin. *Photography:* George Folsey. *Editing:* Barney Rogan. *Music director:* Frank Tours. 8,613 feet. 96 minutes.
CAST: GROUCHO (*Mr. Hammer*); HARPO (*Harpo*); CHICO (*Chico*); ZEPPO (*Jamison*); Margaret Dumont (*Mrs. Potter*); Mary Eaton (*Polly Potter*); Oscar Shaw (*Bob Adams*); Kay Francis (*Penelope*); Cyril Ring (*Harvey Yates*); Basil Ruysdael (*Hennessy*); Sylvan Lee; Gamby-Hale Ballet Girls; Allan K. Foster Girls.
Shot in spring 1929 at Paramount's Astoria Studios on Long Island. Released in the United States August 3, 1929. The MCA-TV print is about four minutes shorter than the original release length.

ANIMAL CRACKERS. 1930. *A* Paramount *picture. Director:* Victor Heerman. *Screenplay:* Morrie Ryskind. *Continuity:* Pierre Collings. *Based on the musical play, book by:* George S. Kaufman and Morrie Ryskind. *Music and lyrics* ("*Hooray for Captain Spaulding*", "*Why Am I So Romantic?*"): Bert Kalmar and Harry Ruby. *Photography:* George Folsey. 8,897 feet. 98 minutes.
CAST: GROUCHO (*Captain Jeffrey T. Spaulding*); HARPO (*The Professor*); CHICO (*Signor Emanuel Ravelli*); ZEPPO (*Horatio Jamison*); Margaret Dumont (*Mrs. Rittenhouse*); Lillian Roth (*Arabella Rittenhouse*); Louis Sorin (*Roscoe W. Chandler*); Hal Thompson (*John Parker*); Margaret Irving (*Mrs. Whitehead*); Kathryn Reece (*Grace Carpenter*); Robert Greig (*Hives the butler*); Edward Metcalf (*Inspector Hennessey*); The Music Masters (*Six footmen*).
Also shot in the East at the Astoria Studios. Released in the United States September 6, 1930.

MONKEY BUSINESS. 1931. *A* Paramount *picture. Director:* Norman McLeod. *Story:* S. J. Perelman and Will B. Johnstone. *Additio-*

179

nal dialogue: Arthur Sheekman. *Photography:* Arthur L. Todd. 77 minutes.

CAST: GROUCHO, HARPO, CHICO, ZEPPO (*The Stowaways*); Thelma Todd (*Lucille*); Rockcliffe Fellowes (*Joe Helton*); Tom Kennedy (*Gibson*): Ruth Hall (*Mary Helton*); Harry Woods (*Alky Briggs*); Ben Taggart (*The Captain*); Otto Fries; Evelyn Pierce; Maxine Castle.

No specific screenplay credit — it seems to have been written by all three writers. This and subsequent films were shot in Hollywood. Released in the United States September 19, 1931.

HORSE FEATHERS. 1932. *A* Paramount *picture. Director:* Norman McLeod. *Screenplay:* Bert Kalmar, Harry Ruby, S. J. Perelman and Will B. Johnstone. *Photography:* Ray June. *Music and lyrics ("I'm Against It", "Everyone Says 'I Love You' "):* Bert Kalmar and Harry Ruby. 68 minutes.

CAST: GROUCHO (*Professor Quincey Adams Wagstaff*); HARPO (*Pinky*); CHICO (*Barovelli*); ZEPPO (*Frank Wagstaff*); Thelma Todd (*Connie Bailey*); David Landau (*Jennings*); Robert Greig (*The Biology Professor*); James Pierce (*Mullen*); Nat Pendleton (*MacHardie*); Reginald Barlow (*Retiring President of Huxley College*); Florine McKinney (*Peggy Carrington*); E. J. LeSaint and E. H. Calvert (*Professors in Wagstaff's study*).

The print released to television by MCA-TV is incomplete (see text — besides which Florine McKinney does not appear). Released in the United States August 19, 1932.

DUCK SOUP. 1933. *A* Paramount *picture. Director:* Leo McCarey. *Screenplay:* Bert Kalmar and Harry Ruby. *Additional dialogue:* Arthur Sheekman and Nat Perrin. *Photography:* Henry Sharp. *Art direction:* Hans Dreier and Wiard B. Ihnen. *Editing:* LeRoy Stone. *Music and lyrics (including "His Excellency Is Due" and "The Country's Going to War"):* Bert Kalmar and Harry Ruby. *Music direction:* Arthur Johnston. 68 or 70 minutes.

CAST: GROUCHO (*Rufus T. Firefly*); HARPO (*Pinkie*); CHICO (*Chicolini*); ZEPPO (*Bob Rolland*); Margaret Dumont (*Mrs. Teasdale*); Louis Calhern (*Ambassador Trentino*); Raquel Torres (*Vera Marcal*); Edgar Kennedy (*The Lemonade Seller*); Edmund Breese (*Zander*); William Worthington (*First Minister of Finance*); Edwin Maxwell (*Secretary of War*); Leonid Kinsky (*Agitator*); Verna Hillie (*Secretary*); George MacQuarrie (*First Judge*); Fred Sullivan (*Second Judge*); Davison Clark (*Second Minister of Finance*); Charles B. Middleton (*Prosecutor*); Eric Mayne (*Third Judge*).

There never was a scene in which Harpo played the harp or Chico played the piano. Released in the United States November 17, 1933.

(In the following films, to save space, only musical numbers which the Marx Brothers performed are included in the credits).

A NIGHT AT THE OPERA. 1935. *A* Metro-Goldwyn-Mayer *picture. Production:* Irving G. Thalberg. *Director:* Sam Wood. *Screenplay:* George S. Kaufman and Morrie Ryskind. *Additional material:* Al Boasberg. *Story:* James Kevin McGuinness. *Photography:* Merritt B. Gerstad. *Art direction:* Cedric Gibbons, Ben Carré and Edwin B. Willis. *Editing:* William LeVanway. *Musical score:* Herbert Stothart. 8,438 feet. 93 minutes.

CAST: GROUCHO (*Otis B. Driftwood*); HARPO (*Tomasso*); CHICO (*Fiorello*); Margaret Dumont (*Mrs. Claypool*); Siegfried Rumann (*Herman Gottlieb*); Kitty Carlisle (*Rosa*); Allan Jones (*Ricardo Baroni*); Walter King (*Rodolpho Lassparri*); Edward Keane (*The Captain*); Robert Emmet O'Connor (*Henderson*); Lorraine Bridges.

Released in the United States November 15, 1935.

A DAY AT THE RACES. 1937. *A* Metro-Goldwyn-Mayer *picture. Production:* Irving G. Thalberg, Sam Wood. *Associate producer:* Max Siegel. *Director:* Sam Wood. *Screenplay:* George Seaton, Robert Pirosh, and George Oppenheimer. *Story:* George Seaton and Robert Pirosh. *Photography:* Joseph Ruttenberg. *Art direction:* Cedric Gibbons, Stan Rogers, and Edwin B. Willis. *Editing:* Frank E. Hull. *Music direction:* Franz Waxman. 9,824 feet. 109 minutes.

CAST: GROUCHO (*Dr. Hugo Z. Hackenbush*); HARPO (*Stuffy*); CHICO (*Toni*); Margaret Dumont (*Mrs. Emily Upjohn*); Siegfried Rumann (*Dr. Leopold X. Steinberg*); Allan Jones (*Gil Stewart*); Maureen O'Sullivan (*Judy Standish*); Douglas Dumbrille (*Morgan*); Leonard Ceeley (*Whitmore*); Esther Muir (*Miss Nora*); Robert Middlemas (*The Sheriff*); Vivien Fay; Ivie Anderson and the Crinoline Choir.

Released in the United States June 11, 1937. Screen Actors Guild 'Best Supporting Actress' Award for 1937 to Margaret Dumont.

ROOM SERVICE. 1938. *An* R.K.O.-Radio *picture.* Pandro S. Berman *in charge of production. Assistant to the producer:* Philip Loeb. *Director:* William A. Seiter. *Screenplay:* Morrie Ryskind. *Based on the stage play by:* John Murray and Allen Boretz. *Photography:* J. Roy Hunt. *Art direction:* Van Nest Polglase and Al Herman. *Set decoration:* Darrell Silvera. *Editing:* George Crone. *Music director:* Roy Webb. 78 minutes.

CAST: GROUCHO (*Gordon Miller*); HARPO (*Faker Englund*); CHICO (*Harry Binelli*); Lucille Ball (*Christine*); Ann Miller (*Hilda Manney*); Frank Albertson (*Leo Davis*); Donald MacBride (*Wagner*); Cliff Dunstan (*Gribble*); Philip Loeb (*Timothy Hogarth*); Alexander

Asro (*Sasha*); Charles Halton (*Dr. Glass*); Philip Wood (*Simon Jenkins*).

Released in the United States September 30, 1938.

AT THE CIRCUS. 1939. *A* Metro-Goldwyn-Mayer *picture. Producer:* Mervyn LeRoy. *Director:* Edward Buzzell. *Screenplay:* Irving Brecher. *Photography:* Leonard M. Smith. *Art direction:* Cedric Gibbons and Stan Rogers. *Set decoration:* Edwin B. Willis. *Editing:* William H. Terhune. *Music direction:* Franz Waxman. *Song "Lydia, the Tattooed Lady", music:* Harold Arlen *lyrics:* E. Y. Harburg. 7,812 feet. 87 minutes.

CAST: GROUCHO (*J. Cheever Loophole*); HARPO (*Punchy*); CHICO (*Antonio Pirelli*); Margaret Dumont (*Mrs. Dukesbury*); Florence Rice (*Julie Randall*); Kenny Baker (*Jeff Wilson*); Eve Arden (*Peerless Pauline*); Nat Pendleton (*Goliath*); Fritz Feld (*Jardinet*); James Burke (*John Carter*); Jerry Marenghi (*Little Professor Atom*); Barnett Parker (*Whitcomb*).

Released in the United States October 20, 1939.

GO WEST. 1940. *A* Metro-Goldwyn-Mayer *picture. Producer:* Jack Cummings. *Director:* Edward Buzzell. *Original screenplay:* Irving Brecher. *Photography:* Leonard Smith. *Art direction:* Cedric Gibbons and Stan Rogers. *Set decoration:* Edwin B. Willis. *Music direction:* Georgie Stoll. *Editing:* Blanche Sewell. *Song "Ridin' the Range", music:* Roger Edens *lyrics:* Gus Kahn. *Harpo's solo "From the Land of the Sky Blue Water" by:* Charles Wakefield Cadman. 7,227 feet. 80 minutes.

CAST: GROUCHO (*S. Quentin Quale*); HARPO (*Rusty Panello*); CHICO (*Joseph Panello*); John Carroll (*Terry Turner*); Diana Lewis (*Eve Wilson*); Robert Barrat (*Red Baxter*); Walter Woolf King (*Mr. Beecher*); June MacCloy (*Lulubelle*); George Lessey (*Railroad President*); **Mitchell Lewis (*Halfbreed*); Tully Marshall (*Dan Wilson*); Harry Tyler (*Telegraph Clerk*); Iris Adrian; Joan Woodbury.**
Released in the United States December 6, 1940.

THE BIG STORE. 1941. *A* Metro-Goldwyn-Mayer *picture. Producer:* Louis K. Sidney. *Director:* Charles Reisner. *Screenplay:* Sid Kuller, Hal Fimberg and Ray Golden. *Story:* Nat Perrin. *Photography:* Charles Lawton. *Art direction:* Cedric Gibbons and Stan Rogers. *Set decoration:* Edwin B. Willis. *Editing:* Conrad A. Nervig. *Music direction:* Georgie Stoll. *Song "Sing While You Sell", music:* Hal Borne *lyrics:* Sid Kuller and Hal Fimberg. 7,492 feet. 83 minutes.

CAST: GROUCHO (*Wolf J. Flywheel*); HARPO (*Wacky*); CHICO

(*Ravelli*); Margaret Dumont (*Martha Phelps*); Douglass Dumbrille (*Mr. Grover*); Tony Martin (*Tommy Rogers*); Virginia Grey (*Joan Sutton*); William Tannen (*Fred Sutton*); Marion Martin (*Peggy Arden*); Virginia O'Brien (*Kitty*); Henry Armetta (*Guiseppi*); Anna Demetrio (*Maria*); Paul Stanton (*George Hastings*); Russell Hicks (*Arthur Hastings*); Bradley Page (*Duke*); Charles Holland.

Released in the United States June 20, 1941.

A NIGHT IN CASABLANCA. 1946. *A* United Artists *release. A* David L. Loew *production. Director:* Archie L. Mayo. *Original screenplay:* Joseph Fields and Roland Kibbee. *Additional material:* Frank Tashlin. *Photography:* James van Trees. *Production designer:* Duncan Cramer. *Set decoration:* Edward Boyle. *Editing:* Gregg G. Tallas. *Music:* Werner Janssen. [*Song "Who's Sorry Now", music and lyrics:* Ted Snyder, Bert Kalmar and Harry Ruby.] 7,655 feet. 85 minutes.

CAST: GROUCHO (*Ronald Kornblow*); HARPO (*Rusty*); CHICO (*Corbaccio*); Sig Ruman (*Count Pfefferman alias Heinrich Stubel*); Lisette Verea (*Beatrice Rheiner*); Charles Drake (*Lt Pierre Delmar*); Lois Collier (*Annette*); Dan Seymour (*Captain Brizzard*); Lewis Russell (*Galoux*); Frederick Gierman (*Kurt*); Harro Mellor (*Emile*); David Hoffman (*Spy*); Hall Harvey (*Smythe*).

Released in the United States May 10, 1946.

LOVE HAPPY. 1949. *A* United Artists *release* (*Great Britain:* Monarch). *Production:* Lester Cowan. *Presented by:* Mary Pickford. *Director:* David Miller. *Screenplay:* Frank Tashlin and Mac Benoff. *Story:* Harpo Marx. *Photography:* William C. Mellor. *Production designer:* Gabriel Scognamillo. *Editing:* Basil Wrangell and Al Joseph. *Music:* Ann Ronell. *Music director:* Paul Smith. 7,694 feet. 85 minutes.

CAST: HARPO (*Harpo*); CHICO (*Faustino the Great*); GROUCHO (*Sam Grunion*); Vera-Ellen (*Maggie Phillips*); Ilona Massey (*Madame Egilichi*); Marion Hutton (*Bunny Dolan*); Raymond Burr (*Alphonse Zoto*); Melville Cooper (*Throckmorton*); Paul Valentine (*Mike Johnson*); Leon Belasco (*Mr. Lyons*); Eric Blore (*Mackinaw*); Bruce Gordon (*Hannibal Zoto*); Marilyn Monroe (*Grunion's client*).

Released in the United States March 3, 1950. Released in Britain around September, 1951.

1924   May 19: Stage show *I'll Say She Is,* scripted by Will B. Johnstone, opened at the Casino and became a roaring success.

1925   Film *Too Many Kisses* appeared with Harpo in a supporting role. This romantic comedy in a Spanish setting had Richard Dix, Frances Howard, Joe Burke, William Powell, Frank Currier, and Paul Panzer billed before Harpo. Details are lacking of how he came to be in this which even seems to pre-date their first real Broadway play.

1925   December 8: Stage play *The Cocoanuts* opened at the Lyric and ran for 375 performances, a full season on Broadway, as well as two years on the road.

c1926   Film *Humorisk* was made privately by the Marxes on the wave of success. A friend raised $ 6,000 and it was made in two weeks at Fort Lee, N. J., studios and in a studio at 49th St. and 10th Ave. in New York. "Harpo played a character named Watson and made his entrance in a high hat, sliding down a coal chute into the basement. The finale showed Groucho, in ball and chain, trudging slowly off into the gloaming." (Kyle Crichton) The picture was never released but a print is said to have survived destruction and other prints to have been made from it.

1928   October 23: Stage play *Animal Crackers* opened at the 44th Street Theater and ran for 191 performances. It was laid off the following summer, went on tour in mid-October.

1929   October: Book by Groucho, *Beds,* was being serialised in the magazine College Humor prior to publication in 1930.

c1934   Half-hour radio show, *Flywheel, Shyster and Flywheel,* written by Arthur Sheekman and Nat Perrin, sponsored by Esso, starred Groucho and Chico, and ran for 26 weeks. Harpo made a triumphant tour of Russia (see his book). Groucho also played straight in a revival of *Twentieth Century.*

1936   M-G-M short in early Technicolor, *La Fiesta de Santa Barbara,* featured Buster Keaton, Leo Carillo, Robert Taylor and Harpo Marx. Harpo's red wig presumably made a fine challenge for the colour process,

1937   Film *The King and the Chorus Girl* was released. Its story — a topical one about a king who married a commoner — was by Groucho and Norman Krasna. Mervyn LeRoy directed Fernand Gravet, Joan Blondell and Edward Everett

Horton in this successful film. In the advertising a small picture of Groucho appeared with the words "He wrote it!"

1937   A Groucho-Chico radio sketch by the late Al Boasberg was found to have infringed a copyright and the two Marxes asked the court's advice on the best prisons.

1939   Radio's *The Kellogg Show* starred Groucho and Chico but stopped at the outbreak of war in Europe.

1941   and 1942: Groucho was a regular guest on *The Rudy Vallee Show*.

1942   Book by Groucho, *Many Happy Returns*, was published.

c1943   Chico headed his own band, did piano solos and lines in Italian dialect.

c1944   Chico appeared alone in the big revue *Take A Bow*. Harpo played in a revival of *The Man Who Came to Dinner* and appeared very briefly in film *Hollywood Canteen*. Groucho started a radio series, *The Pabst Show*, but was replaced by up and coming Danny Kaye.

1947   Film *Copacabana*, directed by Alfred E. Green with Carmen Miranda and Steve Cochran, starred Groucho as Lionel Q. Devereaux, delivering passable wisecracks as a penniless agent in much the *Room Service* situation and reverting briefly to traditional moustache and costume for a spirited rendering of Kalmar and Ruby's number "Go West Young Man" — a glimpse of the old magic.

1948   September 27: Play *Time for Elizabeth* by Norman Krasna and Groucho Marx opened at the Fulton Theater on Broadway and closed after 8 performances. The authors had started writing it in 1941 under the title *Middle Ages*. See bibliography, entry 5.

1950   Film *Mr. Music* featured Groucho as a guest star. A dull, overlong comedy directed by fellow humorist Richard Haydn. Groucho shows up for a student show and performs a comedy song "Life Is So Peculiar", interrupted by a vaudeville routine (Bing Crosby acting as feed).

c1951   In an intriguing piece of casting Harpo was to play Androcles in Chester Erskine's film of Shaw's *Androcles and the Lion* but the studio head Howard Hughes insisted on substituting his discovery Alan Young in the role.

c1951   Groucho started his long-running show *You Bet Your Life*. There were both radio and TV versions which won awards and high ratings. See Chapter 16.

1951   Film *Double Dynamite*, directed by Irving Cummings with Jane Russell and Frank Sinatra, co-starred Groucho as a waiter, Emil J. Kech.

1952   Film *A Girl in Every Port*, directed by Chester Erskine with Marie Wilson and William Bendix, co-starred Groucho.

S. J. Perelman has described a visit to the set in "I'll Always Call You Schnorrer, My African Explorer".

c1953   TV series *College Bowl* featured Chico as the proprietor of an ice-cream parlour and college hang-out. He generally played the piano in each show.

1957   Film *Will Success Spoil Rock Hunter?* (in Britain: *Oh! For a Man!*) produced Groucho as the secret love of the Jayne Mansfield character.

1957   Film *The Story of Mankind,* directed by Irwin Allen from his screenplay with Charles Bennett, featured the Marx Brothers. See Chapter 16.

1958   TV production (Playhouse 90), *Next to No Time,* had Chico as a guest star portraying Mr. Kramer.

1959   March 8: Telecast of *The Incredible Jewel Robbery*, a Revue production directed by Mitchell Leisen, produced by Harry Tugend, written by Dallas Gaultois and James Edmiston, with music by Elmer Bernstein. See Chapter 16.

1959   Book *Groucho and Me* was published — written by Groucho.

1960   April: one-hour colour telecast of *The Mikado* by Gilbert and Sullivan starred Groucho as Koko.

1961   Harpo wrote book *Harpo Speaks!* with Rowland Barber.

1965   Book *Memoirs of a Mangy Lover* by Groucho was published. Groucho also made a series called *Groucho* for British television.

1967   Book *The Groucho Letters* published.

1968   Film *Skidoo*, directed by Otto Preminger, features Groucho as a gang boss.

Appendix III

BIBLIOGRAPHY

A. By and about the Marx Brothers

1. Agee, James, review of *A Night in Casablanca*, in "Agee On Film" (pages 201-2) (New York, McDowell Obolensky; London, Peter Owen, 1963).
2. Ames, D. L. "A Night in Casablanca: a book of the film" (London, Hollywood Publications, 1946). A paperback with some good illustrations based on the original screenplay which differs in several respects from the finished film.
3. Crichton, Kyle, "The Marx Brothers" (London, Heinemann, 1951).
4. Eyles, Allen, "Great Films of the Century: *A Night at the Opera*", in *Films and Filming*, issue of February 1965, pages 16-20.
5. Krasna, Norman, and Marx, Groucho, "Time for Elizabeth" (acting edition) (New York, Dramatists Play Service Inc.) A dull little play about retiring from work to a life of enjoyment only to find work is better. It has a laboured first act and rather obvious construction leading to the predictable. There is no depth of characterisation, no really involved situations, and little that is really funny (at least as read).There are no lines from author Groucho that recall the screen Groucho.
6. Laura, Ernesto G., "Il contributo dei Marx Brothers alla nascita del film comico sonoro", in *Bianco e Nero*, issue of November-December 1964, pages 16-82. Long study of the Marxes' work, with filmography and bibliography.
7. Mannock, Laura, "Full Marx Brothers", in *Picturegoer*, issue of March 1931, pages 12-13. Poor fan-magazine interview with Groucho and Chico, but nice illustrations.
8. Martin, André, "Harpo Marx a n'en plus finir", in *Cinéma 64*, No. 91, December, pages 42-47. Farewell tribute to Harpo.
9. Martin, André, "Les Marx Brothers ont-ils une âme?", in *Cahiers du Cinéma* 44-45-47-48, February, March, May and June issues, 1955. Long, useful and stimulating study of the Marx Brothers with very generous script extracts from *Animal Crack-*

ers and *Monkey Business*. But doesn't deal with every film and has inaccuracies.

10. Marx, Arthur, "Groucho" (London, Victor Gollancz, 1954). Footnotes by Groucho.

11. Marx, Groucho, "Groucho and Me" (New York, Bernard Geis Associates, 1959; London, Victor Gollancz, 1959).

12. —, "Many Happy Returns" (New York, Simon and Schuster, 1942). Advice on the gentle art of income tax evasion. Some very good wit, worth reading.

13. —, "Memoirs Of A Mangy Lover" (New York, Bernard Geis Associates, 1965). Humorous history of love.
    —, "The Groucho Letters" (London, Michael Joseph, 1967). Letters to and from Groucho, with many gems. Edited and introduced by Arthur Sheekman.

14. Marx, Harpo (with Rowland Brown), "Harpo Speaks!" (London, Victor Gollancz, 1961).

15. Olsson, Lars, article on the career of the Marx Brothers with filmography, in *Film rutan* (Sweden), issue No. 4, 1964.

16. Perelman, S. J., "The Winsome Foursome — How to go batty with the Marx Brothers when writing a film called *Monkey Business*", in *Show*, issue of November 1961, pages 34-38.

17. Rosten, Leo, "Groucho: The Man from Marx", in "The Weekend Book of Humour", edited by P. G. Wodehouse and Scott Meredith (London, Herbert Jenkins, 1954; WDL Books, 1960). Humorous appreciation of Groucho. Appeared originally in *Look* magazine.

18. Rowland, Richard, "American Classic", in *The Penguin Film Review* No. 7, London, 1948. A short but well-written and appreciative study of the Marx Bros. from seven of their films. Originally appeared in *Hollywood Quarterly*.

19. Seton, Marie, "Salvador Dali + 3 Marxes", in *Theatre Arts,* issue of October 1939.

20. Tynan, Kenneth, "Groucho, Perelman and Tynan talk about Funny Men", in *The Observer* (London) on June 14, 1964.

21. Whitebait, William, review of *At the Circus,* in *The New Statesman,* issue of December 16, 1939.

22. Woollcott, Alexander, "Portrait of a man with red hair", in *The New Yorker* 4, dated December 1, 1928, pages 33-6.

23. —, "A short history of the magician's daughter who was the managing mother of the four Marx Brothers", in "While Rome Burns". (New York, Viking Press, 1934).

24. —, "A Strong Silent Man", in *Cosmopolitan 96,* dated January 1934, pages 56-7 and 108.

B. *Other references*

25. Brown, John Mason, essay "The Theatre of the Twenties", in "Dramatis Personae" (London, Hamish Hamilton, 1963).
26. Cassandra, "The agony of making people laugh", in *The Daily Mirror* (London), dated Wednesday June 10, 1964, pages 16-7. A meeting with S. J. Perelman.
27. Cerf, Bennett (editor), "An Encyclopedia of Modern American Humor" (New York, Hanover House Doubleday & Co., 1954). "Dr. Kronkhite — A Vaudeville Classic" appears on pages 531-6.
28. Esslin, Martin, "The Theatre of the Absurd" (London, Eyre & Spottiswoode, 1962).
29. Feibleman, James, "In Praise of Comedy, a Study of its Theory and Practice" (London, George Allen & Unwin, 1939).
30. Florey, Robert, "Hollywood d'Hier et d'Aujourd'hui" (Paris, Editions Prisma, 1948) pages 155-7.
31. Highet, Gilbert, "The Anatomy of Satire" (Princeton, N. J., Princeton University Press, and London, Oxford University Press, 1962).
32. Kramer, Dale, "Ross and the New Yorker" (London, Victor Gollancz, 1952).
33. McCarey, Leo, "Leo et les aléas", interviewed by Serge Daney and Jean-Louis Noames, in *Cahiers du Cinéma* 163, issue of February, 1965. Reference to *Duck Soup* on page 17, plus several stills.
    Oppenheimer, George, "The View from the Sixties: Memories of a Spent Life" (New York, David McKay, 1966). Oppenheimer's account of working on the script of *A Day at the Races* contains a substantial indictment of Irving G. Thalberg as having a detrimental influence on the boldness of the Marxes' humour.
34. Roth, Lillian (with Mike Connolly and Gerold Frank), "I'll Cry Tomorrow" (London, Arthur Barker). "It was one step removed from a circus" and other comments about working with the Marx Brothers on *Animal Crackers*.
35. Rovere, Richard, "Senator Joe McCarthy" (London, Methuen, 1960).
36. Weatherby, W. J., "Marxmanship" (from an interview with Billy Wilder), in The Guardian (London), clipping undated.